A FALCON GUIDE®

BASIC ESSENTIALS® SERIES

BASIC ESSENTIALS®
USING GPS

SECOND EDITION

BRUCE GRUBBS

FALCON GUIDE®

GUILFORD, CONNECTICUT
HELENA, MONTANA

AN IMPRINT OF THE GLOBE PEQUOT PRESS

A FALCON GUIDE®

A previous edition of this book was published in 1999 by Falcon Publishing, Inc.

Text and page design by Casey Shain

Library of Congress Cataloging-in-Publication Data

Grubbs, Bruce (Bruce O.)
Using GPS / Bruce Grubbs.-2nd ed.
p. cm. - (Basic essentials)
Includes index.
ISBN 0-7627-3421-3
1. Global Positioning System. I. Title. II. Basic essentials series.

G109.5.G78 2005
910'.285-dc22 2005040339

Manufactured in the United States of America
Second Edition/First Printing

The author and The Globe Pequot Press assume no liability for accidents happening to, or injuries sustained by, readers who engage in the activities described in this book.

Contents

Preface

In this book, I describe how to use the Global Positioning System (GPS) as a practical land navigation tool. The emphasis is on GPS as a supplement to, not a replacement for, classic navigational skills. Remember that GPS is not a substitute for the older land navigation tools (map, compass, and altimeter), for common sense, or for backcountry experience.

I have avoided technical terms as much as possible—but jargon and abbreviations do have their uses. For example, it is easier to refer to the direction toward a landmark as a *bearing* than as *the direction toward a landmark.* I explain all terms as I use them, and I describe GPS techniques in general terms that apply to any receiver. As you read this book, consult your receiver's manual for specific applications of the techniques.

Contact the manufacturers listed in the appendix for up-to-date information on their models. All of the manufacturers have Web sites where you can browse through complete specifications and sometimes download equipment manuals. For those who want to go deeper into global positioning, I have included a chapter on advanced GPS and a recommended reading list in the appendix. This information is not necessary to put GPS to practical use in the outdoors.

CAUTION: Never use GPS, or any other system, as your sole means of navigation. Outdoor recreation activities are by their very nature potentially hazardous. All participants in such activities must assume responsibility for their own actions and safety. The information contained in this book cannot replace sound judgment and good decision-making skills, which help reduce exposure to risk; nor does the scope of this book allow for the disclosure of all potential hazards and risks involved in outdoor recreation activities. Learn as much as possible about the activities you participate in, prepare for the unexpected, and be cautious. The reward will be a safer and more enjoyable experience.

Acknowledgments

I would like to thank longtime friend Jean Rukkila for a fine job of proofreading the first edition of this book. Moreover, special thanks to Duart Martin, who got me started with GPS and then supported this project through its numerous twists and turns. Again, thanks to all the people at Globe Pequot, and especially to Bill Schneider, my patient editor who made this second edition a reality.

Introduction

Halfway into an early spring cross-country ski trip, a sudden mountain storm blots out the sun, the wind picks up, and snowflakes fall steadily. You and your group are in a whiteout. Visibility is only a couple of hundred yards, and blowing snow obscures the horizon. Your ski tracks, shallow to begin with, soon disappear in the drifting snow.

You have a map and compass, as always, so you know that you can use classic route-finding techniques to find your vehicle. To do this, you would use the map to decide what direction to go, then maintain direction by compass. Once at the edge of the plateau, you could follow it to the road, and then follow the road to your car. However, the irregular edge of the plateau and the road would add significant distance to your trip back.

There is a better way. You get your Global Positioning System (GPS) receiver from your pack and turn it on. Within a minute, unaffected by cloud cover, your receiver locks onto the system's navigation satellites and displays your present position, which you save. Using your map, you also enter the position of your vehicle in the receiver. Finally, you set up a route using the two saved positions. Now the receiver tells you the direction and distance to your vehicle. You turn the receiver off but put it in a pocket to keep it handy.

You use your compass to maintain direction as the group sets off. Frequently, you stop and check your progress by turning on the GPS receiver. The map display shows the direction and distance to your car, and it gives a graphic of your location and desired course. When the receiver shows your car a half-mile away, you leave the receiver on—although it is awkward to ski with—because you know that it would be easy to miss the end of the road in the low visibility. As you ski, the GPS display tells you your speed, direction of travel, and estimated time of arrival. Within a few minutes, the receiver's arrival alarm starts to beep and the lead skier spots your vehicle.

What Is GPS?

The Global Positioning System comprises twenty-one active satellites orbiting 12,000 miles above the earth. The satellites' orbits are arranged so that several satellites are always in view from any point on earth. Spare satellites and ground control stations make up the rest of the system. Though the U.S. Department of Defense developed the system for military use, the government makes GPS available to all users without charge. Consequently, GPS is used by businesses to track parcel delivery trucks, by individual motorists to find their way to a specific street address, and by ships and aircraft of all sizes.

This book focuses on handheld GPS receivers that are intended for civilian use and suitable for navigation in the backcountry and in self-propelled sports. An expanding variety of GPS receivers is being manufactured. There are large receivers intended to be mounted permanently in vehicles, tiny ones designed to be imbedded in smaller devices, and credit card–size receivers designed to plug into data-gathering computers. Specialty receivers are made for marine use, aviation, surveying, the earth sciences, and the military.

As its name implies, GPS allows a user to determine position. GPS is unique among the various methods of navigation in that it can determine position very rapidly with a high degree of accuracy, in any weather and at any time of day, anywhere on our planet. Using radio signals transmitted by the satellites, a GPS receiver can determine position to within 50 feet (15 meters). Small, lightweight, inexpensive handheld receivers are available that make GPS a practical means of backcountry navigation. Because the GPS receiver measures position so often, it can calculate your direction and rate of travel. It also can tell you the direction to travel to reach your destination and display this information on a moving map.

Satellite navigation is not magical; several real limitations exist. The receiver must have a clear view of the sky to receive signals from the satellites. The microwave radio signals used travel in straight lines, like light waves, so trees can block the signals, as can high canyon walls.

(Clouds, rain, and snow do not interfere with the satellite signals.) Rarely, poor satellite locations can make it impossible to get a position fix. A GPS receiver is a complex piece of equipment than can fail or be broken, and its batteries can die. In addition, the receiver is helpful only if its user knows how to operate it properly.

GPS must be used in conjunction with the older navigation tools. The position display on a GPS receiver is a meaningless string of numbers without a map to plot your location. Although some GPS receivers do feature moving maps, they do not provide enough detail for you to navigate on foot in rough terrain. Knowing the direction to a favorite spot does not help unless you have a compass to point you in that direction. In addition, a sensitive, temperature-compensated altimeter can read altitude more accurately than a handheld GPS.

How GPS Works

The heart of GPS is precise measurement of time. Each satellite in the system carries several atomic clocks on board. The satellites transmit precisely timed radio signals that are picked up by your GPS receiver. Each signal carries precise timing information, telling the receiver exactly when the signal left the satellite. Using an onboard computer, the receiver measures time in transit—the time required for the radio signal to travel from the satellite to the receiver. The satellites also transmit a navigation signal that gives their exact position. Using this information, your receiver calculates its exact distance from the satellite and places your receiver somewhere on a spherical surface. When your receiver links up with two more satellites and computes its distance from them, the receiver then knows that it is located on the surface of three imaginary spheres. The point at which those spheres intersect is the receiver's position. Acquiring a fourth satellite refines the position calculation so that altitude can be computed.

The GPS satellites in orbit require constant updates that are transmitted from ground control stations. The ground stations continuously track the satellites and calculate updated positions. Corrections are also made for the drift of the atomic clocks. This information is uplinked to the satellites to update the navigation signal. Without this continuous flow of information, the system's accuracy would degrade in a matter of days. The ground stations can also reposition satellites and replace them with orbital spares as necessary.

Navigation Tools

GPS Receivers

A GPS receiver is a sensitive microwave radio receiver combined with a sophisticated computer. Control buttons and a display screen complete the receiver. The technical specifications can be a bit intimidating, and the various units can be somewhat difficult to compare. This chapter describes features that you should consider when searching for a receiver that best meets your specific needs.

Size

You naturally will want the **smallest receiver** that has all of the features you will need. Fortunately, GPS receivers are getting smaller as the technology improves; even wristwatch-size receivers are now available. Remember, however, that smaller receivers have smaller displays, which may make map and navigation screens harder to read. Examine the screen on a receiver before you buy it, or make sure that you can return any receiver you order through the mail or over the Internet.

Weight

Minimal weight is desirable, as long as battery life is adequate. Batteries make up a considerable portion of the weight of a GPS receiver. Weights range from less than three ounces to more than a pound.

Batteries

Battery life varies from four to twenty-four or more hours of continuous use in handheld receivers, using two to four AAA- or AA-size alkaline cells. These figures do not sound practical for extended backcountry trips until you realize that typically the receiver is on for only a few minutes per hour. Even a receiver with a four-hour battery life will last for days in the field. Some receivers also have a battery-saving mode in which position updates occur at a slower-than-normal rate. GPS receivers normally use alkaline batteries, but you may be able to use other types. Lithium cells are lighter than alkaline batteries, last longer, and work better in cold weather. Rechargeable nickel-metal-hydride (NiMH) cells save money, and the best of them last as long per charge as throwaway alkalines.

An **external power connector** allows you to use power from a vehicle or external power pack, which saves the receiver's batteries. Make certain that the receiver input voltage range matches the voltage of the power source. You probably will have to buy a power cable from the manufacturer or a third-party supplier, unless the receiver comes with one.

Waterproofing

Because your GPS receiver will be used in bad weather as well as good, look for some degree of **weatherproofing.** Some receivers are sealed and completely waterproof while others are merely water resistant. Sea kayakers and other boaters should get a completely waterproof receiver. Waterproof dry bags designed for GPS receivers are available; these bags keep the receiver afloat and provide attachment points to your boat or gear.

Temperature Limits

All electronic devices have **minimum and maximum temperature limits** beyond which the device may not function. On GPS receivers, the display may not work in very hot or cold conditions. If you plan to operate in extreme conditions (in deserts in summer or in mountains in winter, for example), make certain that your GPS receiver can handle it. If you plan to use your receiver in cold weather, make sure that you can operate it while wearing gloves. Battery life is shortened by cold, so you may have to run your receiver from an external battery pack kept warm inside your clothing.

Accuracy

The Department of Defense no longer limits the **accuracy** available to civilian users; the standard accuracy is 50 feet horizontally and 75 feet vertically. This is more than accurate enough for backcountry navigation. Positions are displayed to a precision of 3 feet, but do not be fooled into thinking that the receiver is that accurate.

Some receivers have a position-averaging feature that works when you are stationary. This feature averages a series of fixed positions over time, and units that have it claim accuracy of better than 15 feet horizontally. Many GPS receivers also can make use of Wide Area Augmentation System (WAAS) signals to achieve accuracy of better than 15 feet horizontally and 23 feet vertically; this system works regardless of whether you are moving or stationary. See Chapter 12 (Advanced GPS) for more information on WAAS and on GPS accuracy.

Channels

GPS units receive satellite signals through **receiver channels.** A receiver must pick up signals from at least three satellites to determine position and four to calculate both position and altitude. Reception of more satellites improves the receiver's accuracy and allows it to better maintain a lock when satellites are temporarily blocked from view. (A receiver is considered to be "locked" when it is receiving signals from enough satellites to produce a reliable position.) Eight channels should be the minimum; most units receive twelve. Older GPS receivers use a single receiver channel to pick up multiple satellites by scanning four or more satellites in turn, a technique called multiplexing. Because the signals are not received continuously, it is easier for the receiver to lose lock on a satellite. Newer units have separate receivers for up to twelve parallel channels; each channel continuously receives a single satellite. A parallel channel receiver locks on more quickly than a multiplexing receiver and maintains that lock better under varying conditions, such as a partially obstructed sky or rapid changes in direction and speed. Parallel channel receivers have become inexpensive, so avoid multiplexed receivers.

Antennas

Two types of **antennas** are used on handheld GPS receivers: quadrifilar and patch. The quadrifilar is a coil of wire in a rectangular plastic housing that forms a horn-like projection on the top or side of a receiver. Quadrifilar antennas are good at receiving satellites close to the horizon, but are poor at picking up satellites directly overhead. Patch antennas are flat and are built into the top of a receiver. They are better at picking up satellites overhead, but poorer at seeing satellites that are closer than 10 degrees above the horizon. Either type may be fixed, meaning that you have to move the entire receiver to reorient the antenna, or movable, meaning that the antenna can be repositioned independently of the receiver. Movable antennas are more versatile in getting fixes in bad locations, but they also are bulkier. Quadrifilar antennas are often removable, allowing you to mount one on the inside of your vehicle's windshield for better reception. The connecting cable must be kept short because the satellite signals are very weak and get lost in long cables. If you need to mount a GPS antenna further than a few feet from the receiver, you will have to use an amplified antenna to magnify the satellite signals before sending them down the cable.

Measurement Units

Some receivers allow you to change only the overall **measurement unit** system. Others allow you to customize individual displays. For example, you could display distance in nautical miles and elevation in meters. If you have special requirements, be sure that your receiver can be set to use the units you will need.

Coordinate Systems

The GPS receiver displays your position using coordinates—sets of numbers used on maps to accurately specify location. Your receiver must be capable of displaying position with the **coordinate system** used by your map. At a minimum, the receiver should use the latitude/longitude (lat/long) and Universal Transverse Mercator (UTM) coordinate systems. Other coordinate systems may apply in different parts of the world.

Map Datums

A **datum** is a model of the earth's surface based on a surveyed network of physical points. All American-made GPS receivers have the map datums used in North America. If you plan to use your receiver in another country, make sure that the receiver has the appropriate datums. Maps are being converted to the World Geodetic Standard 1984 (WGS84, the GPS mapping standard) worldwide, but this process will take time.

Waypoint Capability

Most GPS receivers can store a hundred or more **waypoints** (landmarks) using short, descriptive names made up of six or more characters and numbers. You probably will want to keep separate notes describing the purpose of your waypoints. A typical GPS receiver can store five or more routes, each containing twenty or more waypoints. Since it is rarely possible to travel in a straight line in the backcountry, for practical use a GPS receiver should be capable of handling routes with at least a dozen waypoints.

Track Logging

The **track-logging** feature allows you to record your actual route as you travel. The receiver does this by automatically storing position fixes in memory, either at preset time intervals or when you make changes in direction or speed. The length of the track-log record is limited by the amount of memory in the receiver—when the memory is full, the oldest track fixes are erased. Most receivers display your track on their plot screen. Track logging is useful for comparing your actual route of travel with your desired route. In addition, many GPS receivers allow you to invert the track log so that you can use it to backtrack to your starting point. With suitable software, some receivers allow you to copy the track log to a computer for mapping and other purposes.

Track logging can be very useful when you explore back roads in a vehicle where external power is available for the receiver. It is not as useful for hiking or other self-propelled activities because the receiver must be left on to record the track, which quickly uses up your batteries.

Memory

The **memory** in a GPS receiver retains user-defined waypoint and route information, as well as various settings such as distance receivers. The more memory the receiver has, the more waypoint and route information it can hold. Check that the receiver has a backup system that maintains the memory long enough to change batteries—otherwise, you will lose all of your stored waypoints and custom settings when the batteries run down.

Speed Limits

A few manufacturers purposely design **speed limits** into their products. For example, one company makes a line of receivers intended for ground navigation and another intended for aircraft navigation. The ground receivers are programmed to stop working when the user is traveling faster than 100 knots (115 miles per hour); this prevents the receivers from being used for air navigation. If you are a pilot who would like to use the same GPS receiver in your plane and on the ground, make sure that the receiver does not have a speed limitation or buy a receiver intended for air navigation.

Database

More expensive receivers have a **built-in database** that houses a list of permanent waypoints. Aviation receivers, for example, usually have databases containing waypoints for airports and navigation aids. You can pick your destination by its name, which saves you the trouble of manually entering the coordinates. Since backcountry users have so many possible destinations, GPS receivers intended for ground use have general databases that list towns and cities, if they have a database at all.

Plot Screen

Nearly all GPS receivers have a **plot screen,** which shows your position in relation to nearby waypoints. You should be able to set the plot screen to north up (so that the top of the screen is always north) and to track up (so that your direction of travel is always toward the top of the screen). You should also be able to zoom in and out, to change the area and detail the plot shows, and to pan the plot to show different areas. Some receivers feature autozoom, which increases the scale of the plot screen as you get closer to a waypoint. Usually, plot screens allow you to enter a new waypoint from a position marker on the screen or to navigate directly to a position selected from the screen.

Area Maps

More sophisticated receivers have graphics capable of showing a map of your surrounding area. This allows the receiver to display a **moving map,** which changes as you move to graphically present your position and direction of travel in relation to surrounding features. Detail shown may include cities, highways, city streets, back roads, rivers, and coastlines. Some receivers allow you to load your own maps from a computer. Even the most detailed moving maps are no substitute for a large-scale topographic map in the backcountry; however, they can be very useful for general navigation, especially in a vehicle, boat, or aircraft. Because it shows your position in relation to surrounding highways and towns, a GPS receiver with a moving map can help you navigate out of the wilderness in an emergency. In the future, as electronic memory becomes cheaper, GPS maps will be able to show more detail.

Displays

Almost all handheld GPS receivers have **liquid crystal display** (LCD) screens, but these vary in quality and readability. The display uses tiny dots called pixels; the more pixels, the more information that can be displayed. Make sure that navigation information is displayed in large, readable characters. Check that the display is readable in dim light, as well as in bright sunlight; a contrast setting should allow you to adjust the display for different light levels. Most receivers have backlit displays that can be turned off to save batteries.

Celestial Data

Many GPS receivers will display **sunrise and sunset data** as well as moon phases, sun azimuth/elevation, and tide information for any waypoint or location, on any date and at any time. This information can be useful for trip planning and outdoor photography.

Simulator Mode

Simulator mode capability allows you to simulate navigation when you are not actually moving. You can manually enter a starting position, heading, and speed. Using the simulator is a great way to learn how to use your receiver, but make certain that the display clearly indicates when the receiver is in simulator mode.

Data Port

A **data port** allows you to connect the receiver to other devices to send and obtain data. You can connect your receiver to a personal computer to enter and maintain more waypoints and routes than the receiver's memory can hold, and you can use such applications as moving maps and other mapping software. A differential GPS receiver can be connected to the data port for increased accuracy. In addition, some GPS receivers will let you copy waypoints and other data to other receivers.

Accessories

Most receivers come with basic **accessories** such as a carrying case. Optional accessories include an external power cord, an external antenna or antenna extension cable, mounting kits, and computer interface kits. You may find a mounting kit useful if you plan to often use your receiver in a vehicle. A computer interface kit allows you to transfer data such as waypoints to and from a computer.

Controls

Handheld receivers have a limited amount of space, so designers use as few **control buttons** as possible. Most receivers feature four buttons or a four-way rocker button that allows the user to move up, down, right, and left through the main pages. A page on a GPS receiver is a screen of information. All of the most-used navigation and input pages should be readily accessible. You can enter characters and numbers by scrolling through the alphabet with the up and down buttons. Less frequently used functions, such as datum and coordinate settings, are usually on a menu page. The best way to decide if you like the controls on a receiver is to try them before buying it. An important item to check is the method used to turn the power on and off; it should be difficult to do so accidentally. Most receivers have a recessed power switch or button.

Accuracy Warning System

A critical feature is the **warning system** that tells you if navigational accuracy is degraded due to poor satellite reception or if there are problems with the receiver itself. Some receivers use icons on the screen as warnings; others beep and display a message.

Flexibility

User-changeable fields are available on most receivers. These fields let you customize the navigation screens to show exactly the data you need. However, all receivers display the important navigation information.

Odometer

Most receivers have an **odometer** display that works the same way the settable odometer does in your car: It accumulates distance from the last time it was reset. The odometer function is most useful for air or water navigation, when you are traveling in straight lines and the receiver can be left on continuously. On roads or trails, the odometer reads lower than the actual distance traveled.

Maps for GPS

A map for GPS navigation must have a coordinate system that allows you to specify locations accurately. The coordinate system is essential to finding your position on the map from the GPS position readout and to determining waypoints to load into the receiver.

Maps are produced with varying amounts of detail and coverage. **Scale** is the ratio of distance on the map to distance on the ground and is the most common way of expressing the amount of detail on a map. For example, a scale of 1:5,000,000 means that 1 inch on the map represents 5,000,000 inches—about 80 miles—on the ground. A scale of 1:24,000 means that 1 inch on the map represents 24,000 inches—2,000 feet—on the ground. The 1:24,000 map can show greater detail than the 1:5,000,000 map, but it covers less area. A map of the United States at a scale of 1:5,000,000 will comfortably fit on a wall but does not have nearly enough detail for backcountry use. Conversely, the 1:24,000 map shows plenty of detail for land navigation on foot, but it covers a very small area—about 7 by 9 miles.

U.S. Geological Survey (USGS) **topographic maps** are the most accurate maps published in the United States. A topographic map uses **contour lines** to show elevation and the shape of the land. A contour line connects points on a map that have the same elevation. "Topo" maps come in various scales; the 7.5-minute series is the largest-scale map and has the most detail. These maps cover an area of about 63 square miles at a scale of 1:24,000.

The U.S. Forest Service (USFS) and other land management agencies such as the Bureau of Land Management (BLM) also publish maps useful for backcountry navigation. The most commonly available maps are visitor maps, usually printed at a scale of 1:126,720, or 0.5 inch to the mile. These usually cover a major portion of a national forest or other land management area. Newer visitor maps are topographic, but most of the maps in print are still planimetric; in other words, they do not show elevation. They do show the official agency road network, including road numbers, and are very useful for finding your way to the trailhead. Lat/long is usually the primary coordinate system on these maps. Positions can be measured down to 0.1 mile or so, which is accurate enough to specify the location of a trailhead or road intersection in your GPS receiver.

Several companies produce private recreational maps. These vary in scale and accuracy but often are more up to date on roads, trails, and recreational facilities than are government maps. Some do not have coordinate systems, however.

Grid and Latitude/Longitude Readers

Although not essential, a Universal Transverse Mercator grid reader makes it easier to determine waypoints on a map. If you prefer to work with latitude and longitude, a lat/long reader is essential. You must use a grid reader or a lat/long reader designed for the scale of map that you are working with. Both types are printed on clear plastic and may be combined on one reader, at several different map scales. (An example is the Topo Companion, which has UTM and lat/long readers for all of the USGS topographic map scales. See the appendix for ordering sources.)

Compasses

A good compass is essential for backcountry navigation. Because compasses point to magnetic north and maps use true north, it is useful to have a compass that can be adjusted for declination (see Chapter 3). Better compasses have a small screw or other adjustment that lets you dial in the declination, essentially converting the compass to a true-north device. Because the amount of declination varies from place to place, you must set the compass before heading to a new area. An orienteering-style compass with a clear plastic baseplate is also useful; it can be used to lay out bearings on a map, eliminating the need for you to carry a separate protractor. Newer models have UTM scales on their baseplate. Some GPS receivers have built-in magnetic compasses; remember, however, that the compass will fail if the batteries die.

Altimeters

An accurate temperature-compensated altimeter measures elevation to 30 feet, which is more accurate than a GPS receiver. Altimeters are essentially barometers that measure atmospheric pressure; because pressure changes with the weather, an altimeter must be set to a known elevation every few hours during use. You can use GPS and a large-scale topographic map to set your altimeter: Use the GPS to determine your position, then read your elevation from the map. To set your altimeter, always use the elevation from the map, never the GPS readout of elevation. Some GPS receivers have built-in barometric altimeters.

Navigation Skills

Map and Compass Review

Learning to read a map is easier if you orient the map to line up with the terrain. There are three ways to do this: (1) Use a compass to determine north (see below), and turn the map so that its north agrees with the compass; (2) if you are on a linear feature such as a road or trail, turn the map until the same feature on the map is lined up with it; or (3) if you can see one or more distant, known landmarks, turn the map until your position and the landmark's position on the map are lined up with the real thing. Once your map is oriented, you can relate landmark symbols on the map with actual landmarks in the countryside.

To find your direction or orient your maps, you need to know how to use a compass. You will be working with **bearings** (also called azimuths or directions)—the direction from one position to another, measured in degrees clockwise from north. North is 000 degrees, east is 090 degrees, south is 180 degrees, and west is 270 degrees. Bearings can be expressed relative to **true north** or to **magnetic north.** True north is the direction of the geographic North Pole, the axis about which the earth spins. Magnetic north is the direction a compass points as the needle aligns itself with the earth's geomagnetic field. The difference between magnetic north and true north is called **declination.** Declination in the continental United States varies between about 25 degrees east in Washington State to about 20 degrees west in Maine. It changes slowly over time because of changes in the earth's magnetic field. As of this book's date of publication, declination was printed on the margins of U.S. Geological Survey (USGS) maps.

To convert a true bearing to a magnetic bearing, subtract east declination or add west declination. Reverse this procedure to convert from magnetic to true. It is easy to make a mistake in this process, so it is simpler to always work with true bearings because all good maps are printed with true north up.

Remember to stay well away from iron or steel objects, such as vehicles, when using a compass. The larger the mass of metal, the farther you should be from it. For example, you should stand 50 feet from a car or truck and 3 feet from a small object such as a pocketknife.

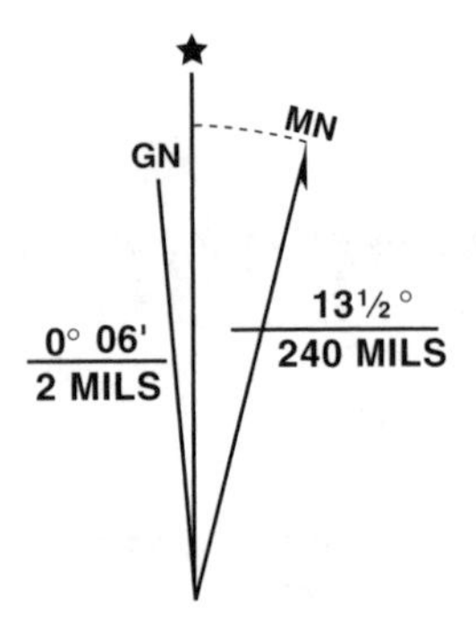

UTM GRID AND 1972 MAGNETIC NORTH DECLINATION AT CENTER OF SHEET

GPS Settings

You should establish a number of settings in your GPS receiver before using it in the field. These settings are usually found under the setup menu.

Most GPS receivers give you several different **mode choices,** including simulator, battery saver, and normal. Simulator mode does not show your actual position and is useful mainly for practicing at home. You do not want to be in simulator mode if you are trying to navigate. Battery-saver mode is the best for backpacking or other extended trips that will have minimal power sources. Normal mode is necessary for using the track-logging and backtrack features; it should be your choice if you are not worried about conserving batteries.

A bonus of carrying a GPS receiver is the availability of accurate time. While it is on, the receiver synchronizes its clock with the accurate clocks on the satellites. Known technically as **GPS time,** the time shown on the receiver is within a few seconds of the world standard time, Universal Time Coordinated (UTC). On most receivers you can change the displayed time to your local time zone by determining the offset from UTC for your time zone. Check your receiver's manual for specific instructions.

Also make sure that your receiver is set to the proper **units of measure.** Most receivers can be set to statute, nautical, or metric units. Some receivers allow you to change only the overall unit system. Because statute miles ("mi" or "sm" on your screen) are the standard units of distance on land in the United States, you normally will use statute units for backcountry navigation. (Unqualified references to "miles" always mean statute miles.) Nautical miles ("nm" on your screen) are slightly longer than statute miles and are used primarily for sea and air navigation. If you paddle a sea kayak or sail, you will be using coastal marine charts and will want to set your receiver to nautical miles. Land navigation in most other countries uses kilometers ("km" on your screen), so you will need to set your receiver to metric units if you are abroad.

You can set the GPS receiver to use either **true north** or **magnetic north;** for land navigation using topographic maps, true north is easier to use.

You also may have several options for setting your **screen orientation.** Most GPS receivers have options that include north up and track. North up is the most useful for navigating in the field because the screen orientation is always the same.

Every map that is accurate enough for navigation is based on horizontal and vertical **map datums.** A datum is a model of the earth's surface based on a surveyed network of physical points. In North America the most common datum on paper maps is the North American Datum of 1927 (NAD27), which is used on USGS maps, U.S. Forest Service (USFS) maps, and many other government and private maps based on them. Other regions of the world have their own datums; more than a hundred are in use.

You must set the GPS receiver to the same datum used by your map; otherwise, position errors will result. The receiver always stores positions internally based on World Geodetic Standard 1984 (WGS84) datum and converts positions to the user-selected datum for display. If you select the wrong datum, the displayed position can be off by as much as a mile. Before starting to work with a map, set the correct datum in your receiver. The datum should be printed in the margin of the map. If it is not, it is probably safe to use NAD27 in North America. Your receiver may break NAD27 into separate datums for the continental United States (CONUS), Alaska, Canada, etc. In this case, select NAD27 CONUS if you are in one of the forty-eight continental states. Most recreational maps are based on USGS maps and use NAD27. Aeronautical charts and some newer maps, as well as most digital maps for GPS and computers, use WGS84. Outside North America, there are many local datums; setting the wrong datum may result in large errors.

You also must set the GPS receiver to the **coordinate system** used by your map before entering waypoints or plotting GPS positions on the map. Fortunately, there are just two common systems in North America: Universal Transverse Mercator (UTM) and latitude/longitude (lat/long).

Latitude and Longitude

The most universal coordinate system is **latitude and longitude,** which can be used to describe positions anywhere on earth. Latitude is the distance north or south of the equator measured in degrees from 0 to 90, with 0 at the equator and 90 north at the North Pole. Longitude is the distance east or west of the prime meridian (located in Greenwich, England) measured in degrees. A degree is 1/360th of a circle; in this case, the circle is the circumference of the earth. Latitude and longitude are usually expressed in degrees, minutes, and seconds. A minute is 1/60th of a degree, and a second is 1/60th of a minute.

For example, the airport at Helena, Montana, is located at 46 degrees 36 minutes 24 seconds north latitude, and 111 degrees 58 minutes 54 seconds west longitude. This position is written as N46° 36' 24" W111° 58' 54". Decimal minutes can be used instead of seconds; the same position would then read N46° 36.40' W111° 58.90'. Rarely, decimal degrees will be used, as in N46.6000° W111.9900°. Most GPS receivers can be set to display positions in any of these formats.

Although lat/long is found on nearly all good maps, it can be difficult

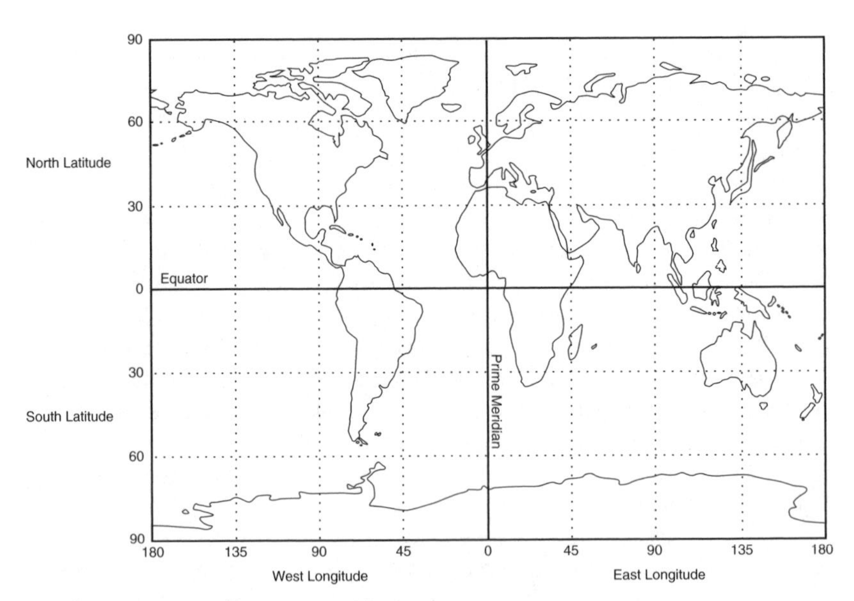

Latitude and longitude

to work with. The problem is that one minute of longitude varies from a distance of 1 nautical mile at the equator to zero at the poles, so the distance between longitude reference lines changes on maps of different latitudes. A special lat/long reader can help you make sense of paper maps; readers are available for common map scales. Computer-based maps are much easier to interpret; you just point and click to get the lat/long coordinates.

Universal Transverse Mercator

Universal Transverse Mercator is a more useful coordinate system for land navigation. UTM uses distances from standard reference points to grid maps into 1,000-meter intervals (1,000 meters = 1 kilometer = 0.62 mile). These squares remain the same at all latitudes covered by the system, so it is easy to read positions on the map. UTM breaks the world into sixty zones, each 6 degrees east to west, and then specifies position in meters north of the equator and east from the prime **meridian** of the zone. (A meridian is a north-south line of reference.) The position of the prime meridian is defined as 500,000 meters east to start with, so that all coordinates have positive numbers. A zone letter is used to break the zones into 8-degree blocks of latitude but is not necessary to specify position.

For example, to specify the location of the Helena airport to the nearest meter (3.3 feet), the coordinates are 12 **424**802mE **5161**726mN. Here "12" is the zone, "**424**802" is the **easting** (to the right on your map), and "**5161**726" is the **northing** (to the north on your map). This means that the airport is located 424,802 meters east of the zone 12 reference meridian and 5,161,726 meters north of the equator. You can use any level of precision. If you wanted to specify the location of the Helena airport only to the nearest 1,000 meters, you would drop the last three digits of the easting and northing and write it as 12 **424 5161.**

UTM does not cover the entire planet; it stops at 84 degrees north and 80 degrees south. (If you are a polar explorer, you can use the Universal Polar Stereographic grid system.) Because the 1,000-meter grids are squares overlaid on the curved surface of the earth, the grid lines are not exactly aligned with true north except at the prime meridian, and the discrepancy can be several degrees. The difference from true north is called grid declination and is printed on the margin of USGS maps. Do not use UTM grid lines as true north reference lines unless you correct for grid declination.

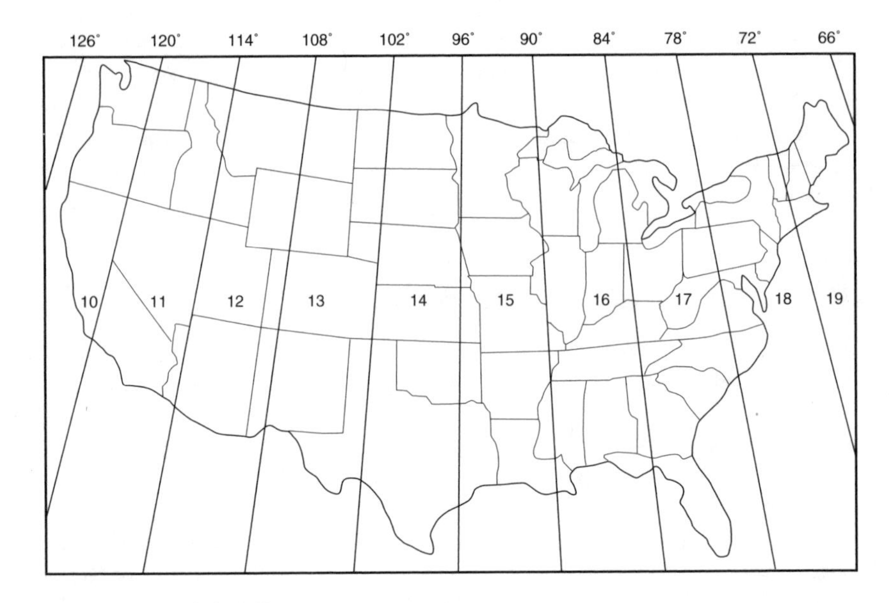

UTM grid zones for the U.S.

Lat/long and UTM references are included on the margins of USGS maps. Some of these maps are overlaid with a light gray UTM grid in 1,000-meter intervals. Unlike lat/long, the UTM grid does not change with latitude, so it can be used to easily measure positions on the map. A UTM grid reader or any convenient straightedge, such as another map, can be used to measure position down to 10 meters on a large-scale map.

Many other grid systems are used in different parts of the world. For example, topographic maps in Great Britain use the British Grid, and Swiss maps use the Swiss Grid. Both of these systems are metric grids similar to the UTM grid, but they have different origin points. Luckily, the same UTM principles apply to all metric grid systems.

Finding Waypoints

To describe the location of a landmark (such as a trailhead, trail junction, creek crossing, or mountaintop) in terms that a GPS receiver can use, you create a waypoint. (Some GPS manufacturers refer to a *landmark* instead of *waypoint,* but the latter is considered the more exact term and is used throughout this book.) A waypoint is simply a point on the map that corresponds to a unique location on the ground, one that is useful for navigation.

In GPS and in other forms of electronic navigation, waypoints are specified in terms of coordinates and can be located anywhere. Normally you create a waypoint by reading the coordinates from a map or by saving your current location in the receiver; however, you can specify one waypoint relative to another or obtain waypoints from a guidebook, friend, or Web page.

When you combine more than one waypoint, you determine a route—a path between two waypoints. Starting and ending waypoints can be used to define a route, and additional waypoints can be used to define turning points or intermediate goals.

Preparing Your Maps

Whether you plan to work with Universal Transverse Mercator (UTM) or latitude/longitude (lat/long), it helps to prepare maps at home. Either for trip planning or in the field, there are a few steps you can take to make it easier to use coordinates. Some U.S. Geological Survey (USGS) maps, for example, do not have UTM grids overlaid on the map, only tick marks along the margins. Pregridding the map makes it easier to use UTM.

Pregridding a USGS Map with UTM Grids

Using a long ruler, carefully draw a grid on the map, connecting the UTM tick marks. On 7.5-minute topographic maps, these are the blue tick marks spaced 1,000 meters (1 kilometer) apart. Use a pencil or fine-point waterproof pen, and draw lightly so that you do not cover any important information on the map.

Pregridding a USGS Map with Lat/Long Grids

Using a long ruler, carefully draw in the meridians and parallels between the lat/long tick marks in the margin. You can locate the lat/long tick marks by looking for minutes and seconds (47' 30", for example). On the USGS 7.5-minute maps, there are tick marks every 2.5 minutes, so you will end up with two parallels and two meridians that divide the map into nine blocks.

Finding a Waypoint with a UTM Grid and UTM Grid Reader

1. Make sure you that are using the correct grid reader for the map scale. For this example we will determine the UTM coordinates of Aspen Spring on the Dane Canyon, Arizona, 7.5-minute USGS topographic map.
2. Place the zero point (the upper right corner) of the UTM grid reader on Aspen Spring.
3. Align the scales on the grid reader with the grid lines on the map.
4. Read 260 meters along the top scale of the UTM grid reader at the nearest 1,000-meter grid line to the west.
5. Append 260 meters to the 1,000-meter grid number, which is 482, to get 482260, the easting.
6. Read 120 meters north where the scale on the right side crosses the nearest 1,000-meter grid line to the south, which is the 3816 grid line.
7. Append 120 meters to 3816 to get 3816120, which is the northing.
8. Refer to the bottom left edge of the map to get UTM Zone 12. The full UTM coordinate for Aspen Spring is 12 4**82**260mE 38**16**120mN. You do not enter "mE" or "mN" into the receiver; therefore these coordinates would read 12 S 4**82**260 38**16**120 on the display. (The "S" is the zone letter, which the receiver calculates from the northing. You do not need to enter it yourself. Note that the 1,000s and 10,000s digits [**82** and **16**] are written in bold, or larger numbers, to make the coordinate easier to read.)

9. Enter the waypoint into your receiver. On most receivers you simply go to the waypoint page or pick the waypoint list from a menu. The waypoint page may have a "new" function that presents a blank waypoint when selected. Enter the waypoint name by using the up and down arrow keys to select the letters and/or numbers; use the left and right arrow keys to move to other character positions. Enter the coordinates the same way. Call this waypoint ASPEN.

Finding a Waypoint without a UTM Grid and UTM Grid Reader

1. Use a long straightedge (in the field, the edge of another map works well) to draw a short section of grid line from the nearest 1,000-meter tick marks to the south.
2. Use the nearest 1,000-meter tick marks to the west to draw another short section of grid line. (The idea is to define the nearest 1,000-meter corner to the southwest of your waypoint.)
3. Use your straightedge to draw your waypoint to the top or bottom edge of the map. Keep the straightedge parallel to the UTM grid by observing the tick marks on both margins.
4. Measure the distance in meters to the nearest UTM tick mark to the west (left).
5. USGS maps have a kilometer and meter scale printed on the margin that you can read to the nearest 10 meters. Use a piece of paper to transfer the distance from the map margin to the scale. Add this figure to the value printed at the tick mark to get the easting.
6. Repeat the procedure using the left and right margins to get the northing.
7. Enter the waypoint into your GPS receiver.

Whatever method you use, read UTM coordinates to the nearest 10 meters when working with a 7.5-minute map so that you can use the full accuracy of your receiver. GPS errors are cumulative, so you want to minimize any source of errors.

3753 III SE
(LONG VALLEY)

UNITED STATES
DEPARTMENT OF THE INTERIOR
GEOLOGICAL SURVEY

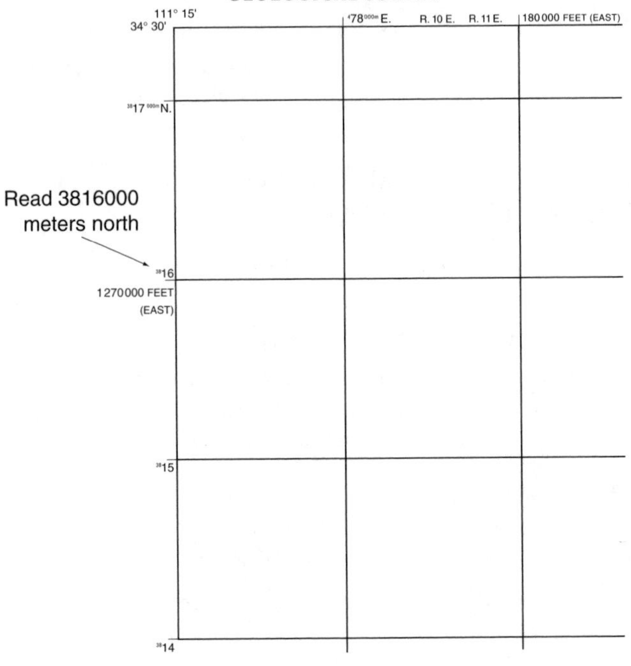

T. 12. N.
34° 22' 30"
111° 15'
478

(PAYSON NORTH)
3762 IV SE

Mapped by the U. S. Forest Service
Edited and published by the Geological Survey
Control by USGS, USC&GS and USFS
Topography by photogrammetric methods from aerial photography taken 1965. Field checked by USGS 1972
Projection: Arizona coordinate system, central zone (transverse Mercator)
10,000-foot grid ticks based on Arizona coordinate system, central and east zones
1000-meter Universal Transverse Mercator grid ticks zone 12, shown in blue. 1927 North American datum
To place on the predicted North American datum 1983 move the projection lines 63 meters east as shown by dashed corner ticks
there may be private inholdings within the boundaries of the national or State reservations shown on this map
Where omitted, land lines have not been established

Read Zone 12

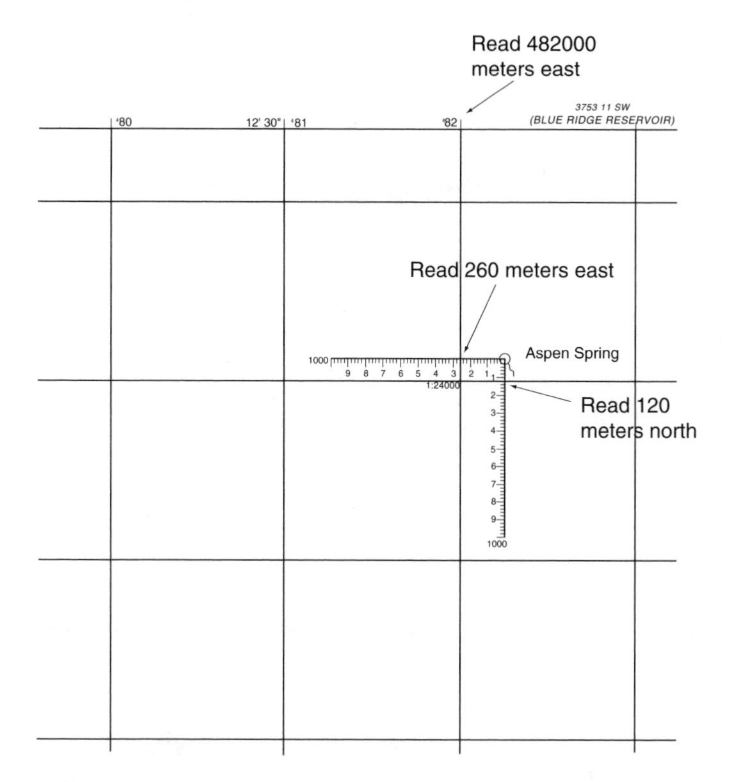

(map detail deleted for clarity)

Determining a UTM waypoint with a grid reader

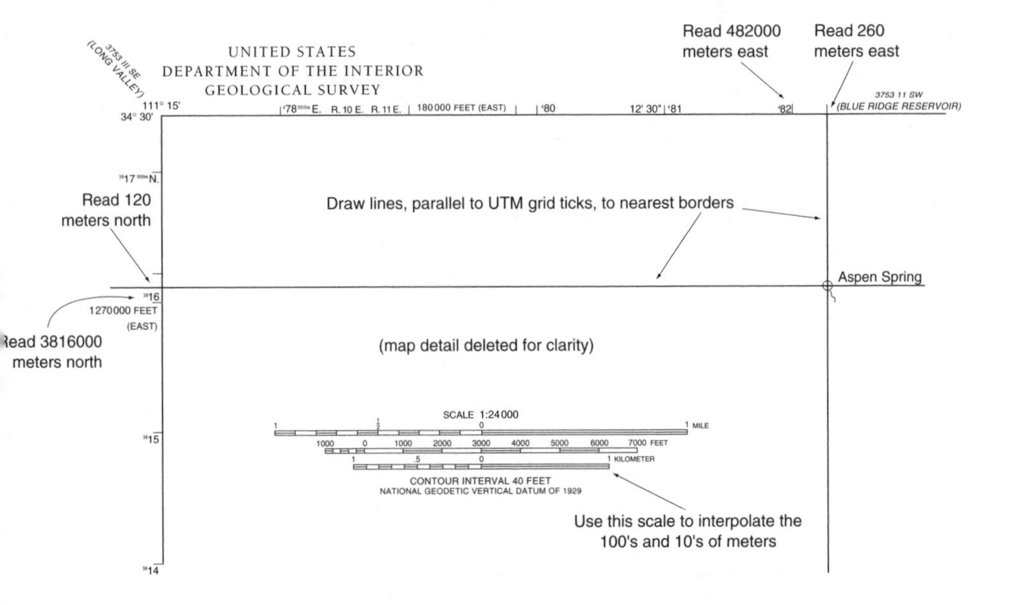

Determining a UTM waypoint without a grid reader

Finding a Lat/Long Waypoint with a Lat/Long Scale

For accurate work with latitude and longitude, you will need a lat/long scale. For this example we will find the lat/long of Dane Spring, on the Dane Canyon quad.

1. Latitude is read using the scale vertically, with the bottom of the scale on the lower parallel. Notice that there are two sets of numbers on the scale. Because the latitude (and longitude) ticks are 2.5 minutes apart on the 7.5-minute series maps, the bottom of the scale may be on a parallel at 00 or 30 seconds (0.5 minute). If the parallel is at 00 seconds, use the (00) numbers. In this case the parallel at the bottom of the scale is at 34 degrees 27 minutes 30 seconds, so use the numbers that start with 30. Read up the scale to Dane Spring at 00. This puts the spring exactly 30 seconds north of the parallel, which makes the latitude N34° 28' 00" or north 34 degrees 28 minutes 00 seconds.

2. Longitude is measured with the base of the scale on the meridian to the right, which in this case is the neatline (the edge of the detail area of the map). Because longitude minutes are shorter than latitude minutes on this map, the scale has to lie at a slant so that the top will lie on the next meridian to the left. Move the scale up or down until it crosses your waypoint; then make sure that the ends are still on their meridians. Again, because the neatline is at longitude 111 degrees 07 minutes 30 seconds, use the numbers that start with 30. Reading to the left, pass 00, which is 111 degrees 08 minutes, and then read 55 seconds at Dane Spring. This makes the longitude W111° 08' 55", or west 111 degrees 8 minutes 55 seconds.

3. Your lat/long waypoint is N34° 28' 00" W111° 08' 55". Enter this waypoint into your receiver as DANESP.

Defining a Waypoint from a Known Waypoint

You can also define a new waypoint using distance and direction from a waypoint already in the receiver. Using Dane Spring as our known waypoint, we can create a new waypoint at McClintock Spring. For this example we will use an orienteering compass with a clear baseplate, but you could use a ruler and a protractor.

1. Put one corner of the compass baseplate at Dane Spring, and then align the edge of the baseplate with McClintock Spring.

2. Turn the compass capsule until the north lines are parallel to a meridian or the neatline. Now you can read the true bearing, 352 degrees, at the lubber line next to the scale on the capsule. (The lubber line is the reference mark on the compass where bearings are read.)

3. Make sure that either Dane or McClintock Spring is at the zero point on the baseplate scale. In this case Dane Spring is at zero, so read 9.2 centimeters at McClintock Spring.

4. Move the compass to the mileage scale at the bottom of the map, and read 1.6 miles at 9.2 cm on the baseplate scale.

5. Define the new waypoint in your GPS receiver by entering the name of the reference waypoint, DANESP, and then the distance and direction. Call the new waypoint MCCLNT.

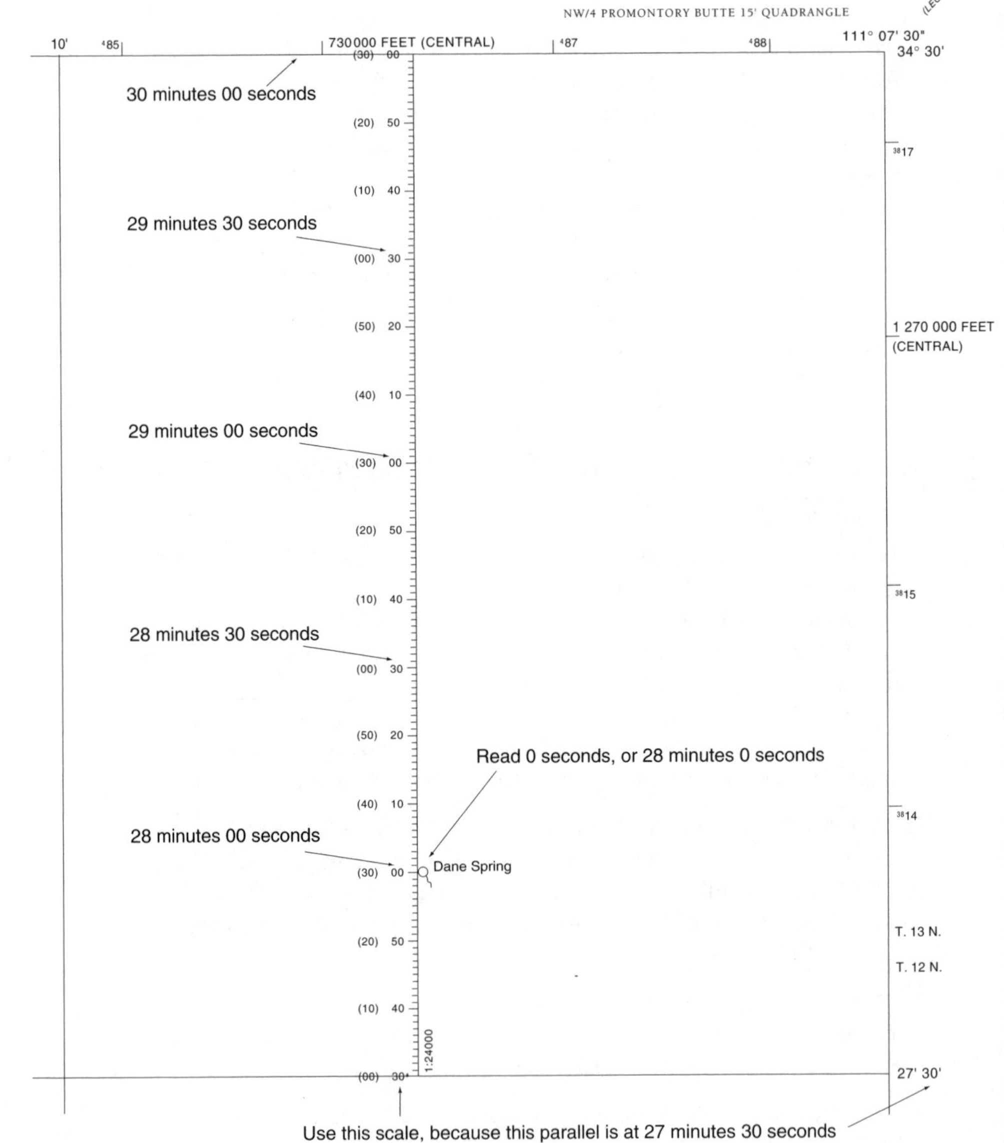

Finding latitude with a lat/long scale

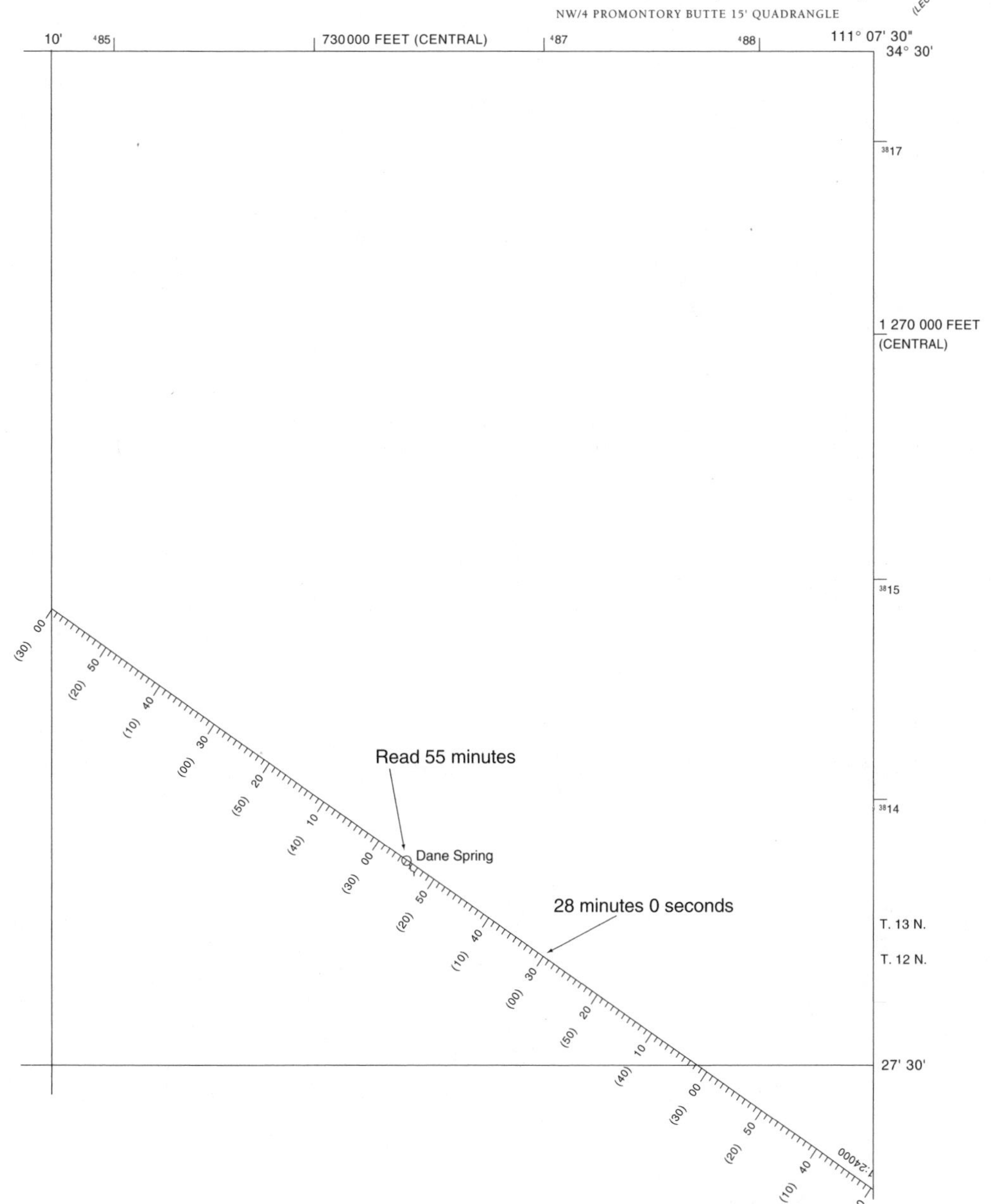

Finding longitude with a lat/long scale

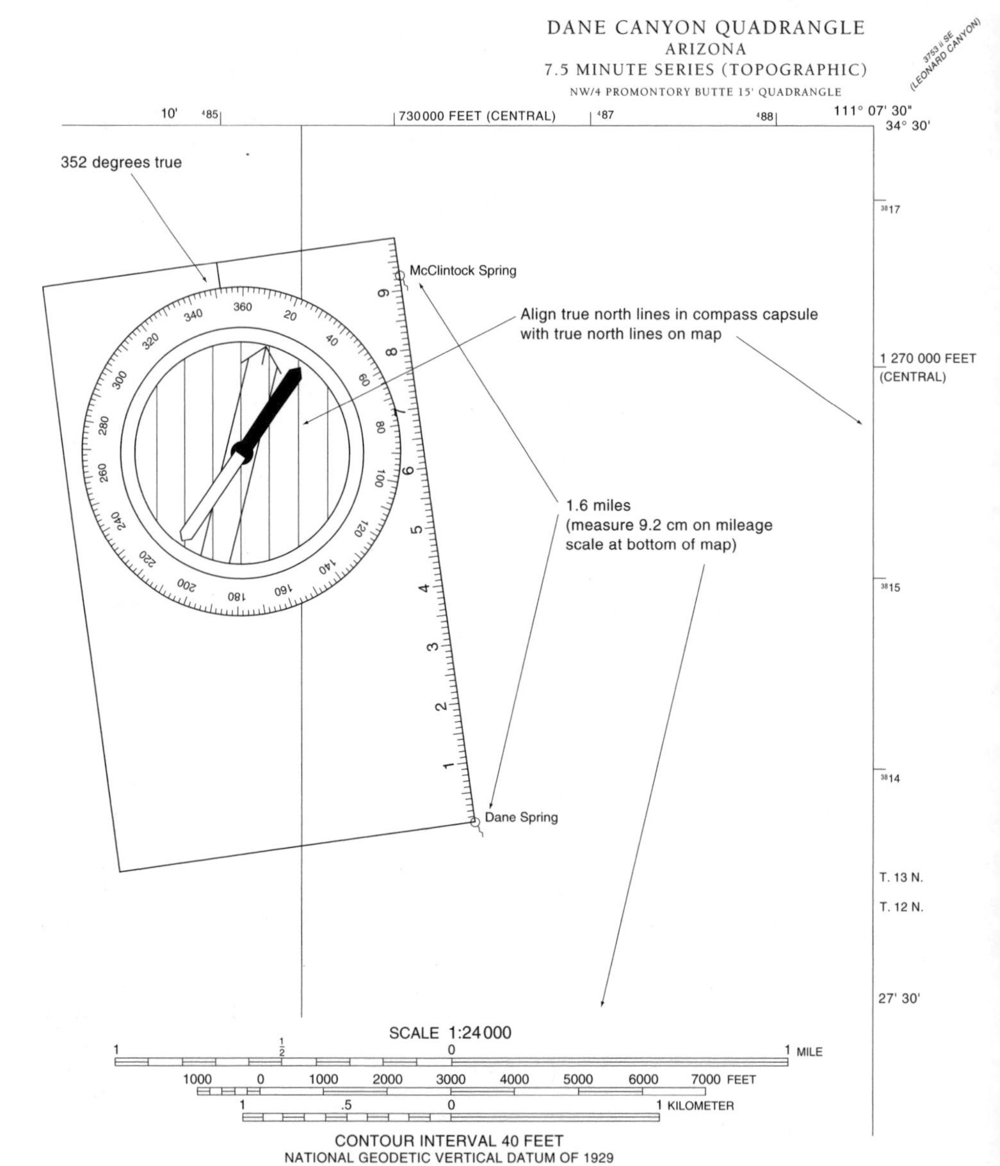

Defining a new waypoint

In field use, you often can estimate coordinates by estimating the position of a map landmark in relation to the coordinate grid or tick marks. This technique is especially useful in bad weather or when you do not have a UTM grid reader or lat/long scale. It also works well when you know your position via conventional navigation but want to use your GPS receiver to confirm it. You can read the coordinates from the receiver's position screen and estimate their location on your map. Always check a new waypoint for reasonableness by noting its distance and direction from an existing waypoint. Incorrectly entering a digit or two can put a waypoint hundreds or thousands of miles away from its correct location. It is easy to spot an error of this magnitude, but it is harder to catch an error of only a mile or so.

PC Mapping

GPS mapping uses a GPS receiver and a personal computer to store, manipulate, and present GPS data. Such systems can function as a very accurate moving map and can be used to navigate to street addresses or businesses. Data can be collected in the field and used to map the location of roads or trails easily and accurately. GPS mapping was once the realm of professional users because of the expensive hardware and required software, but several inexpensive GPS mapping products now bring this capability to general users. These products are based on digital USGS topographic data, which allows the software to compute and display exact coordinates and elevations for any position on the computer screen. Once you have experienced the ease of creating, uploading, and downloading waypoints with a computer, it is hard to go back to a standalone GPS unit. See the appendix for a list of companies that produce mapping software, and refer to Chapter 10 for a practical example of using a computer with GPS.

Field Technique

When you use a GPS receiver in a vehicle, run the receiver on the vehicle's power if possible. Use an external antenna for best results; most come with suction cups to mount on the inside of the windshield, giving the antenna maximum view of the sky. If you do not have an external antenna, keep the receiver near a window, preferably the front windshield. If you are driving, it is safest to have a passenger hold the receiver and do the navigation.

If you are hiking, skiing, paddling, or cycling and run the receiver on its batteries, leave the receiver off unless you need it to find your position or to navigate. Use the battery-saver mode if your receiver has one, and avoid leaving the backlight on continuously. Always carry enough spare batteries to last the trip.

Use all means of navigation at your disposal, not just GPS. On a trail, for example, pay attention to trail signs and use your map to keep track of prominent landmarks. Take notes in a small notebook or on your map as you progress. When hiking cross-country, chart your progress on the map with a pencil. If you save GPS waypoints, write the coordinates or the name of each waypoint on the map or in your notebook.

Determining Your Position

If you are in a vehicle and you are not using an external antenna, you may have to stop and use the receiver outside. Get the best possible view of the sky from your location. In dense forest, find a clearing or opening in the canopy. Stay away from cliffs—they may reflect the satellite signals and cause false readings.

When first turned on, the receiver displays a status page that tells you how many satellites are visible and how strong their signals are. The visible satellite display is usually a small map of the sky, with the horizon represented by the outer ring of a circle and the 45-degree elevation above the horizon represented by an inner circle. Each satellite is marked with a unique number, and reversing the display colors indicates the satellites being received. A satellite is considered visible when it is above the masking angle (normally, 10 degrees above the horizon). A separate display gives the signal strength of each satellite by its number.

The GPS receiver must receive at least four satellites to calculate your position accurately. The position of the satellites is important. GPS position fixes are most accurate when three of the satellites are just above the masking angle, spread evenly along the horizon, and a fourth satellite is directly overhead. GPS positions are least accurate when the four satellites are close together in the sky—a condition called poor satellite geometry. Most receivers provide some indication of the accuracy of the fix. Some use a warning icon to indicate poor satellite geometry; others display a numerical value, such as feet, to indicate the accuracy level.

If you have not used the receiver for several months or have moved several hundred miles since the last use, it may take five to fifteen minutes to get a fix. This is because the almanac data showing the approximate positions of the satellites is out of date. The receiver updates this information from the satellite transmissions. Most receivers allow you to enter an approximate position (the nearest city, for example) to help speed up the process. This option is usually called initialization or sky search.

If you have used the GPS receiver recently but not within the last thirty minutes, it will perform a cold start. This means that the receiver has to wait for the satellites to broadcast their ephemeris data, which gives their precise locations. This happens quickly; most receivers will get a fix within a minute or two from a cold start. A warm start is the fastest of all. If you have used the receiver in the last thirty minutes, it will get a fix in fifteen seconds to a minute.

If there are any sky obstructions, it helps to be stationary when getting a fix. Otherwise momentary interruptions in the signal may make the entire almanac or ephemeris message invalid, forcing the GPS receiver to start over. Parallel channel receivers are faster than multiplexing receivers in getting the first fix. They also maintain their lock better when moving.

Once the GPS receiver has enough satellites for a fix, it will switch to the position page, which shows your current position and usually your altitude and the time. If you are moving, the position page on most receivers also shows your track (your heading or actual direction of travel) and your speed. The position page may also show a compass rose or tape to help you visualize your heading. If the GPS receiver cannot receive at least four satellites, it will display a warning that it is doing 2-D navigation and may ask you to enter your altitude. Do not rely on 2-D navigation unless you are going to be at a constant, known elevation, such as on water. Some GPS receivers do not allow you to enter an altitude and will assume that you are at sea level or use the last computed altitude. Errors of several miles can result from using 2-D navigation on land.

The receiver will start 3-D navigation as soon as it receives four satellites. Some receivers do not display obvious warnings that they are in 2-D mode. It is essential that you know how to determine whether your receiver is in 2-D or 3-D mode.

Occasionally you will have problems fixing a position. The receiver will warn you on the display, possibly with an audible alarm. The usual cause is a poor view of the sky. Because the satellite signals are received strictly by line of sight, even widely spaced trees can block reception. Deep, narrow canyons are especially difficult spots from which to fix your position. The best locations are open meadows or clearings with low horizons. If you have to get a fix in forest cover, move around to get the strongest signal strengths on the status page. Once you do have a fix, do not move until you have saved your position or checked the bearing to your next waypoint, especially if there are overhead obstacles. Occasionally you will not be able to get a fix at all. Wait a few minutes; satellite movement may eliminate the problem. Sometimes turning the receiver off and on again will reset it, and it will lock on.

Finding Your Position on a Map

To find your position on a map with coordinates from your GPS receiver, reverse the procedures described earlier for reading coordinates from a map. If possible, cross-check the GPS position with other means of finding your location, such as nearby landmarks, roads, or trail signs. If circumstances make GPS your only means of navigation (in cases of fog, featureless terrain, or whiteout conditions), take GPS fixes more often and compare them to each other. Remember: Never depend on a single, unverified GPS position in a critical situation.

Some newer GPS receivers have a position-averaging feature that improves accuracy by averaging a series of fixes over time. Accuracy of 15 feet or better is claimed. To use this feature, you must be stationary.

Saving Your Position as a Waypoint

You can save your current position as a waypoint any time the receiver is locked on. Most receivers give you the option of naming the waypoint yourself or letting the receiver automatically assign a name. If you choose the latter, the receiver assigns sequential numbers to waypoints as you enter them. Some receivers also stamp waypoints with the date and time, which can help you remember the purpose of a waypoint later. The automatic feature is useful if you are in a hurry, but in most cases, it is best to name waypoints yourself. GPS receivers allow six to fourteen characters for the name; most have a longer description field. You may want to make notes on your map or in a small notebook to describe the waypoint more fully than you can in the receiver's memory.

The datum and coordinate settings do not matter when you create a waypoint by saving your current position, because the receiver always uses the World Geodetic Standard 1984 (WGS84) to save positions. The receiver converts from WGS84 to the currently selected datum and coordinate systems to display your current position and the location of waypoints. That is why it is critical for you to set the correct datum and coordinate system when plotting coordinates on a map or when reading coordinates from a map for entry into the receiver.

Navigating to a Waypoint

To navigate to a waypoint, use the receiver's GoTo function to select the desired waypoint. The receiver will immediately start navigating from your present position to the chosen waypoint, giving you a choice of several pages of navigation information. The primary page to use while navigating, naturally enough, is the navigation page. (Some receivers have several different navigation pages, each showing different combinations of information. Often one or more of these pages is customizable.) The navigation page shows bearing and distance to the next waypoint from your present position, and your track and speed. If you are exactly on course, your track and the bearing to the waypoint will be the same. Of course, if you are driving on a road, you have to stay with the road system. Still, the track information shows whether your current road is taking you in the general direction of your destination. When you reach a crossroads, the bearing tells you which way to turn.

Another item on the navigation page is the estimated time en route (ETE) to the waypoint. Some receivers also show the estimated time of arrival (ETA) at the waypoint. ETE and ETA are computed from the speed you are traveling toward a waypoint. This is called velocity made good (VMG). As you travel, following a road or trail or dodging obstacles, you are not always headed directly toward the next waypoint. Thus, your rate of progress toward a waypoint is less than your ground speed (your actual speed across the ground). As your actual track (track made good, or TMG) twists and turns, your VMG and ETA change. Some GPS receivers allow you to average velocity over a short period. If yours does not, you can check the ETA occasionally and average it in your head. This knowledge can be useful in figuring out, for example, whether you will be able to drive to a trailhead before dark. If you were planning to camp at the trailhead but your ETA shows that you will not make it before nightfall, you might want to look for a closer place to camp.

Most GPS receivers have a plot page that shows your position in relation to waypoints. Your course (also called the desired track, or DTK) is shown as a straight line from waypoint to waypoint along your current leg. Your TMG is also shown as you progress. Often, bearing and distance to the next waypoint are shown, along with heading (your current direction of travel) and speed. The plot page gives you an easy-to-understand graphic of your navigation. On many receivers a database of geographic information allows the plot to show major roads and cities, as well as other features. Aviation and marine GPS receivers have specialized databases showing airports, navigation stations, and other information useful for navigating in air or on water. These databases allow the receiver to present a true moving map.

As you progress, the display updates the navigation information at least once per second. The GPS receiver will display a warning on the screen when you are approaching a waypoint. Most receivers can be set to give an audible warning as well.

At low speeds (under 10 to 15 miles per hour), GPS receivers may not compute speed consistently due to the accuracy limits of the GPS system. If the displayed speed and ETA fluctuate as you move, you have to either average them in your head or ignore them. Some receivers have an averaging function to smooth out the ETA calculation, making them more useful at low speeds. Still, the best way to navigate at slow speeds (when walking, bicycling, paddling, or skiing, for example) is to use the receiver while stopped. Get a position fix, save it as a waypoint if necessary, note the bearing and distance to the next waypoint, and then shut off the receiver. Use your compass, the sun, or the lay of the land to determine your direction, and then use landmarks or the compass to maintain that direction as you travel.

A good way to practice navigating to a waypoint is to look for benchmarks and other survey marks in the field. When ground surveys are done, the survey points are precisely located and permanently marked with a monument that usually consists of a brass cap about 3 inches in diameter. The plate is set in a concrete post or rock outcrop. The location of survey marks is shown on USGS topographic maps. Benchmarks are used as reference points for mapping and are shown as a small cross or a triangle labeled with "BM" or "VABM" and an elevation.

Trail Hiking

Before leaving a trailhead, always save your vehicle's position as a waypoint and name it something unmistakable, such as TRUCK or TRAILH. That way you will be able to find your way back to your vehicle, even without a map.

It is difficult to use a GPS receiver as you travel. The receiver must be held in a position where its antenna can see the sky. The normal twists and turns of the hiking trail can cause the receiver to lose its lock. For surveying, mapping, and other specialized work, a pack-mounted antenna will overcome these difficulties. A more practical approach for backcountry users is to stop and take a fix periodically. This technique also saves batteries. Rest stops are an ideal time; you can get an updated fix and check the bearing and direction to your next waypoint. This is also a good time to cross-check your position on the map using both the GPS fix and the map and compass fix.

On the trail it helps to have predefined waypoints and routes that you set up at home or at camp before the trip. Of course, you can enter new waypoints at any time using your map and the methods described earlier or by saving your position as a waypoint. In the field, especially in bad weather, it may be easier to define a new waypoint using distance and direction from an existing waypoint.

Even if you do not plan to actively navigate using your GPS receiver, save waypoints at important trail junctions and landmarks such as stream crossings, passes, and campsites. That way you will have additional GPS navigation information if you lose the trail or become disoriented.

Cross-Country Hiking

When cross-country hiking, generally you will select the same waypoints you would use without a GPS receiver. For example, you might plan to hike a trail for a few miles, then strike off cross-country to a good fishing lake. In this case, set up waypoints at the trailhead, the point at which you will leave the trail, and the lake. Then create a route using these three waypoints. As you hike, stop when you feel the need and check your progress with the GPS receiver. As you near the point where you will leave the trail, you may want to leave the receiver on so that you do not miss the turnoff. When the receiver detects that you have reached the turnoff, it will automatically navigate to the next waypoint—in this case, the lake.

Handling Detours

Hiking cross-country usually requires you to continually make small detours to avoid obstacles. The classic navigation technique is to pick a distant landmark in the direction you need to go and travel toward it. You should do this as a backup to GPS, but it will not work in dense forest or fog, of course. The GPS receiver effectively replaces the distant visual landmark with an electronic one. Each time you turn on the receiver, it tells you the direction to your next waypoint from your current position, no matter how much you have deviated from the straight-line course. It also shows you how far off course you are, and in which direction.

Backtracking

The route-reversal feature on most GPS receivers makes backtracking easier. In the example above, reversing the route creates a route from the lake to the trailhead, with an intermediate waypoint at the location where you will rejoin the trail. Some receivers let you create a route from the automatically stored track data. This function works only if you have left the receiver on continuously or have at least gotten fixes at major turns in the route.

Triangulation with GPS

Triangulation can be used with the GPS receiver, map, and compass to identify an unknown landmark that you cannot reach—for example, a distant mountain peak that you would like to identify. First, determine your position with the receiver and mark it on your map. Using the compass, take a bearing on the landmark; plot it on your map by drawing a line from your present position to the landmark. Now travel far enough so that you are looking at the unknown landmark from a different angle—the closer to 90 degrees you are from the first position, the better. Use the GPS receiver to get your new position, and mark it on the map. Take another compass sight on the landmark, and plot the bearing line on the map. The two lines will intersect at the landmark.

Hiking the Cabin Loop

Let's say that you want to find Pinchot Cabin, a trailhead and historic cabin near East Clear Creek in the forested Mogollon Plateau country of central Arizona. From there you want to hike three historic trails in a loop. This chapter shows you how to: (1) set up the necessary waypoints and routes in advance, and (2) use your GPS receiver to successfully navigate the roads and trails on your trip.

Planning the Drive to Pinchot Cabin

All routes must have a starting and ending waypoint, and you will need intermediate waypoints unless you plan to travel in a straight line. Most GPS receivers can store several routes, each consisting of multiple waypoints. Also, routes can be reversed for the return trip so that you do not have to reenter the route data to backtrack.

A **route-editing** feature allows you to edit an existing route and add, change, or delete waypoints. The route-editing screen usually shows the direction and distance to each waypoint from the preceding one as well as the total distance of the route. This is valuable information for trip planning even if you do not actually use the GPS to navigate. (Keep in mind that the total distance shown on the route screen is shorter than the actual road or trail distance on the ground.) Moreover, most receivers remember an active route even when they are turned off; they resume navigating the route the next time they are turned on.

To create the driving route to Pinchot Cabin, look at a map to find your start and end points: the turnoff from Arizona Highway 87 and the historic cabin, respectively. Enter them in the receiver. Then enter a waypoint for each major road junction between the highway turnoff and your destination.

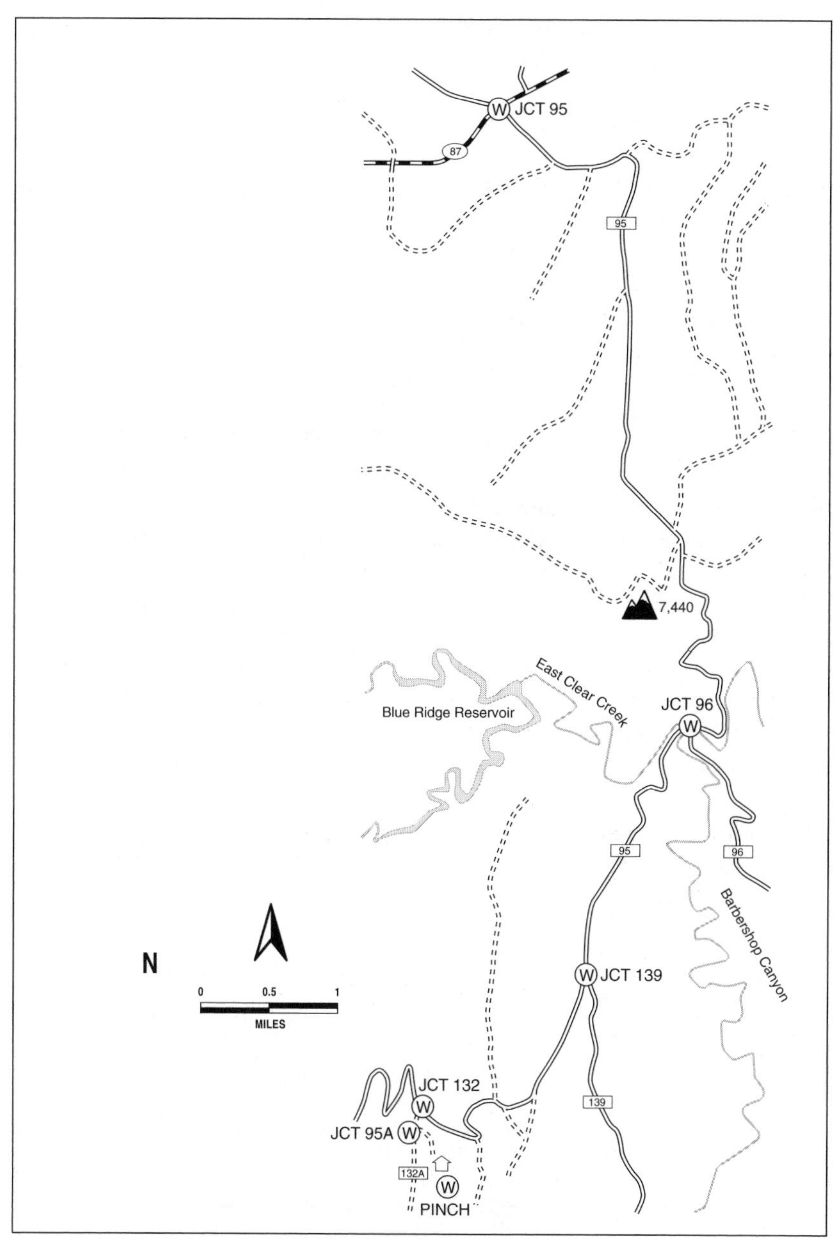

Driving route to trailhead marked with GPS waypoints

Next, define the route using the waypoints you just entered. If your receiver presents a blank waypoint field, scroll through characters with the up/down arrow keys to spell out the waypoint you want. (The right arrow key should move your cursor to the next character position.) Most receivers show the first waypoint that matches the characters you have entered so far. You also can scroll through an alphabetical list of waypoints. Some receivers have a "nearest waypoint" list that sorts waypoints by category or symbol. (Aviation receivers, for example, allow you to look at airport or navigation aid waypoints.) Once you have established the route, name it AZ87-PINCHOT.

```
ROUTE: 1
AZ87-PINCHOT
NO WAYPNT DTK DIS
1. JCT95
              163 4.6
2. JCT96
              201 2.0
3. JCT139
              235 1.4
4. JCT132
              179 0.1
5. JCT95A
              153 0.2
6. PINCH
7. ______     ___ ___
```

Waypoints on the road to Pinchot Cabin

If this route involved a loop with a **cherrystem** (a section of the route traveled both ways), the GPS receiver might get confused and be unable to tell whether you are outbound or inbound. To avoid ambiguity in such situations, break the route into two parts in the receiver. End the first route partway around the loop section, and start the second route with the last waypoint of the first route.

DRIVING ROUTE TO PINCHOT CABIN

Waypoint	Action
JCT95	Turn right onto Forest Road 95, a maintained dirt road
JCT96	Turn right to stay on FR 95
JCT139	Go straight ahead, remaining on FR 95
JCT132	Turn left on Forest Road 132, which may or may not be maintained
JCT95A	Turn left again on Forest Road 95A, the unmaintained spur road to the cabin
PINCH	Historic cabin

Planning the Cabin Loop Hike

You are ready to plan a hiking route on the Cabin Loop trails, which start from Pinchot Cabin. This system of recently retraced U.S. Forest Service (USFS) trails follows the route of three historic trails that date from pioneer days.

You know from talking to an experienced friend that the route can be hard to find. The terrain is a pine-forested plateau cut by numerous shallow canyons. The broad ridges between the canyons have been logged in the past and are laced with a network of forest roads. In some places the route follows old roads, and in other places, it follows blazes on the trees. The trail is distinct in some sections but faint or nonexistent in others. Due to the length of the loop, you plan to do it as an overnight hike, allowing plenty of time for the approach drive and time to explore the historic sites along the route. Because most of the canyons are dry, it is important that you find the springs along the route. You would also like to find the historic cabins and the old trail construction at the canyon crossings.

Before leaving home you use the two U.S. Geological Survey (USGS) topographic maps of the area, Dane Canyon and Blue Ridge Reservoir, to outline the trails as well as you can. With a Universal Transverse Mercator (UTM) grid reader, you create waypoints at the critical points and then name them appropriately. You also make notes to remind yourself of each waypoint's purpose once you are in the field.

The first waypoint you enter is PINCH; it marks the trailhead near Pinchot Cabin, the first historic site. During the hike you will be able to gauge your progress around the loop by checking the distance and direction to PINCH. The next waypoint, BARBER, marks the point where the U-Bar Trail crosses Barbershop Canyon. You know that the section of trail leading to Barbershop Canyon is actually just an easy-to-lose line of tree blazes in the forest. You want to make sure you find the crossing, which has a fine example of the original trail construction dating from more than a hundred years ago.

Beyond the crossing the trail intermittently follows several roads and then passes McClintock Spring. You put a waypoint, MCCLNT, at the spring. Next, the trail crosses Dane Canyon, another historic section of the old trail. There is permanent water flow here, so you mark the location with the DANECN waypoint. Now the U-Bar Trail turns south along the rim of Dane Canyon, passing Dane Spring and the ruins of another old cabin. You mark the spring with another waypoint: DANESP. About 2 miles farther south, the U-Bar Trail ends at its junction with the Barbershop Trail, near Coyote Spring. You name this junction COYOTE.

CABIN LOOP HIKE ROUTE

Waypoint	Action
PINCH	Pinchot Cabin and the trailhead
BARBER	Barbershop Canyon; cross and look for historic trail construction on both sides
MCCLNT	McClintock Spring, a possible water source; exact route of trail not known in this area
DANECN	Dane Canyon; permanent water and historic trail construction here
DANESP	Old cabin and possible water source; should be an access road to this point
COYOTE	Junction with Barbershop Trail; go left for side trip to Buck Springs Cabin; on return, look for Coyote Spring a few yards west
BUCK	Buck Springs Cabin and spring
BARSPR	Barbershop Spring; pick up water here and plan to camp a short distance beyond
HBTR	Junction with Houston Brothers Trail; turn right
HDRAW	Houston Draw; trail crosses a road and descends; must find correct draw
ASPEN	Historic spring
PINCH	Pinchot Cabin and the trailhead

Here you want to take a short side trip to Buck Springs Cabin, less than a mile to the east, and find a nearby spring. You mark the site with a waypoint called BUCK.

The main hike continues west along the Barbershop Trail, which crosses the heads of several canyons. The most important of these is Barbershop Canyon. Though you expect the canyon to be dry at this point, Barbershop Spring is located a few hundred yards west of the main drainage. This spring is important because you may not find water again until near the trailhead. You mark the spring with the BARSPR waypoint. Less than a mile beyond the spring, you cross a dirt road and then meet the Houston Brothers Trail. Because this will be your return trail, you mark it with the HBTR waypoint.

The trail turns north along Telephone Ridge, paralleling the road, and then crosses a branch road and drops into shallow Houston Draw. To stay on the historic route, you must start down into the correct drainage, so you mark this waypoint with the name HDRAW. You place your final waypoint at Aspen Spring and call it ASPEN. When you pass the spring, you will be about a mile from the trailhead at PINCH.

Finally, you use all of the waypoints to create a route named CABIN LOOP, which reads PINCH, BARBER, MCCLNT, DANECN, DANESP, COYOTE, BUCK, COYOTE, BARSPR, HBTR, HDRAW, ASPEN, and PINCH. Note that COYOTE is entered twice because you will backtrack after BUCK. Because the hike is a loop, PINCH is the route's starting and ending waypoint.

Driving to the Pinchot Cabin Trailhead

It is time to use the waypoints and route that you created earlier to find Pinchot Cabin via the Forest Road (FR) system. After setting up the external antenna and connecting your GPS receiver to a power source, you turn on the receiver. Assuming that you have some miles to go to reach the highway turnoff (waypoint JCT95), you use the GoTo function and the navigation page to track your progress toward the junction.

You use a highway map and a forest map to navigate to the turnoff, but the GPS display provides useful information as you drive. Knowing the bearing and distance to JCT95 allows you to gauge your progress. Your track should generally be the same as the bearing, allowing for twists and turns in the road. A large discrepancy in your track might mean that you have taken a wrong turn. The estimated time of arrival (ETA) at the turnoff is based on your present rate of travel. The ETA changes constantly as your track and speed change, so you will need to average it over time. You check your velocity made good (VMG) to see how fast you are actually traveling toward JCT95.

The most useful piece of information that the receiver provides is the distance to the waypoint. When you get within a mile or so, you know to start watching for the turnoff. Most receivers have an arrival alarm that sounds or flashes to signal that you are approaching the destination waypoint. An audible alarm is especially useful if you do not have a passenger to navigate for you.

After turning right onto FR 95, you activate the AZ87-PINCHOT route. The receiver detects that you are between the JCT95 and JCT96 waypoints and correctly assumes that you want to navigate from JCT95 to JCT96. Again, you gauge your progress using the navigation page. The plot or map screen shows your actual track as you follow the road and the desired track from JCT95 to JCT96. You know that the next turn will be onto a maintained road, so you ignore all of the minor side roads.

The arrival alarm warns that you are approaching JCT96, and the receiver says that you are 250 feet from it. (Most receivers change miles to feet when you near a waypoint.) There are no road signs at the junction. Stopping to check your notes, you see that you should turn right. The navigation page on the GPS receiver has jumped to the next waypoint, JCT139, and it gives a bearing of 202 degrees. Your current track is 162 degrees, confirming that you should turn right. Some navigation pages will let you display turn information, which the receiver automatically computes as the difference between the bearing to the waypoint and your actual track. Your turn display says you should turn 40 degrees right. The forest map agrees, so you turn right and continue.

At the next road junction, JCT139, the receiver tells you to turn 34 degrees right. Your notes say to go straight ahead to remain on FR 95. You continue to go straight and follow FR 95 as it curves right.

When you reach the next waypoint, JCT132, you know from your notes and the GPS receiver to turn left. You do not know whether FR 132 is a major or minor road, or if it is signed. In addition, the map shows quite a few side roads in the area, and you know that you are close to the cabin. To make it easier to navigate to the cabin, you switch to the plot page and zoom the display to 0.5 mile. Now you can clearly see your present position at JCT132 and the final two waypoints, including the cabin. FR 132 turns out to be an unmarked minor road; you turn left.

You know that the next turnoff, waypoint JCT95A, is an obscure, unsigned road, so you watch the receiver carefully, find the turnoff, and go left. Now the receiver shows that the cabin is just 0.2 mile ahead. The road winds down a slope into a shallow draw, and there on the edge of a meadow is the old cabin.

Hiking the Cabin Loop

At the Pinchot Cabin trailhead, you switch on the receiver and allow it extra time to get a good fix. You use the position-averaging feature to make sure that the trailhead fix is as accurate as possible, and then you save a waypoint as TRAILH.

Next you check the accuracy of the PINCH waypoint that you entered at home. (In most receivers you can do this by selecting the waypoint from the waypoint list.) The waypoint page shows the coordinates of the waypoint, but more importantly, it shows the bearing and distance to the waypoint from your current position. In this case it shows that you are 105 feet from PINCH, which is well within the 0.06-mile accuracy limits of GPS. As another check, you look at the TRAILH waypoint that you just saved. It shows a distance of 250 feet, still within the accuracy limits. You now have two waypoints marked at the trailhead that you can use to find your way back, if necessary.

You activate the CABIN LOOP route that you created earlier. Switching to the plot page, you change the scale so that you can see the entire route. This serves as double confirmation that you did not enter any waypoints incorrectly. If a waypoint was off by a large amount, it would be obvious on the plot screen. You zoom the map to the 5-mile scale, which shows the next waypoint, BARBER. In doing so you notice that the screen is cluttered by the track you made on the drive to the trailhead, so you use the "clear track" function from the receiver's menu to erase the old track. Now the only lines on the plot screen are the desired track lines between waypoints on the Cabin Loop.

With the GPS receiver turned off but handy in its case on your belt, you start up the U-Bar Trail. It climbs up the east side of the draw onto the forested plateau. The tread is distinct, and you note the blazes on the trees. Before long the trail merges with an old road; you follow the road, keeping an eye out for blazes. Another road soon joins from the left, and a few yards farther on, the tree blazes suddenly veer left, away from the road. There is no sign of trail tread on the flat, needle-carpeted forest floor. You turn on the GPS and check the direction to BARBER. Judging by the sun, the blazes look as if they are headed in the right direction, but you get out your compass and check the bearing to BARBER to confirm. As a precaution, you save your current position as a waypoint, letting the receiver automatically name it 001. You note the waypoint on your topographic map. This waypoint will allow you to find this junction again—the last place where you knew you were definitely on the trail.

Turning the receiver off, you follow the blazes east through the pine forest. The route crosses a major drainage, and about half an hour later, a major dirt road shown on the map. You follow the blazes for a short distance, then lose them in an area of freshly downed trees. You check the receiver for the bearing and distance to BARBER. You are less than half a mile from the canyon crossing. Anxious to find the trail again so that you do not miss the trail construction in Barbershop Canyon, you use your compass to walk the bearing to BARBER. Soon you reach the rim of the small canyon. There is no sign of the trail. Checking the receiver again, you see that BARBER is upstream, or south, of your location. You decide to walk the rim to see if you will intercept the trail. Sure enough, you find the blazed route again and obvious trail construction. You mark this spot as waypoint 002, making a note on your map to remind you of its purpose.

The trail is clear as it descends into the canyon. At the bottom you take a rest break by the stream and check your position with the receiver. The BARBER waypoint is only 150 feet from your location, so you do not need to save a new waypoint. After a while you follow the trail as it climbs out the east side of the canyon. The blazes are easy to follow even after the trail construction disappears on the pine flats. It is less than a mile to McClintock Spring, so you keep an eye on the time. After half an hour, you will have traveled a mile and should be near the spring, so you stop and check the receiver. It is now navigating to MCCLNT, the next waypoint on the route. It shows the spring bearing east at 89 degrees true and 0.3 mile away. The trail, however, is heading southeast at 140 degrees. Leaving the receiver on, you walk along the trail until the spring bears 45 degrees and is 0.25 mile away. It becomes clear that the spring is a short distance from the trail but not actually on it.

Deciding to find the spring and refill your water bottles, you save a waypoint to mark your location and name it PACK. You leave your pack beside a blazed tree but take the GPS receiver, map, and compass. You walk northeast through the forest and find the spring in less than fifteen minutes. After filling your bottles, you activate GoTo navigation to PACK and note the bearing, 227 degrees, and the distance, 0.28 mile. Using the sun to estimate the direction, you walk southwest to return to your pack.

You continue along the trail, following it across Dane Canyon and then south along the rim. The trail is distinct in this section, but you are concerned that you might miss the old cabin at Dane Spring if it is not on the trail, as was the case with McClintock Spring. You check the receiver after about forty-five minutes of walking, and it shows DANESP 0.45 mile distant at a bearing of 168 degrees. Your compass shows that the trail is heading almost directly toward the spring, at 166 degrees, so you expect to find it very near the trail (unless the trail turns). Sure enough, after another twenty minutes of walking, you find the spring and the old cabin ruins at the end of a spur road that meets the trail.

Continuing along the U-Bar Trail as it heads south, you occasionally use the receiver to check your progress toward the next waypoint, COYOTE. You would like to reach the spring near the junction with the Barbershop Trail in time for lunch. You reach the trail junction and find the spring a couple of hundred yards to the west. After lunch you leave your pack and follow the trail east to Buck Springs Cabin, which you find without difficulty. After exploring the cabin and nearby spring, you check your position with the receiver and find that the BUCK waypoint is correct. You hike back to your pack and continue east on the Barbershop Trail.

The trail, now mostly just a line of blazed trees, wanders through an area of shallow draws laced with numerous old roads. Finally, you lose

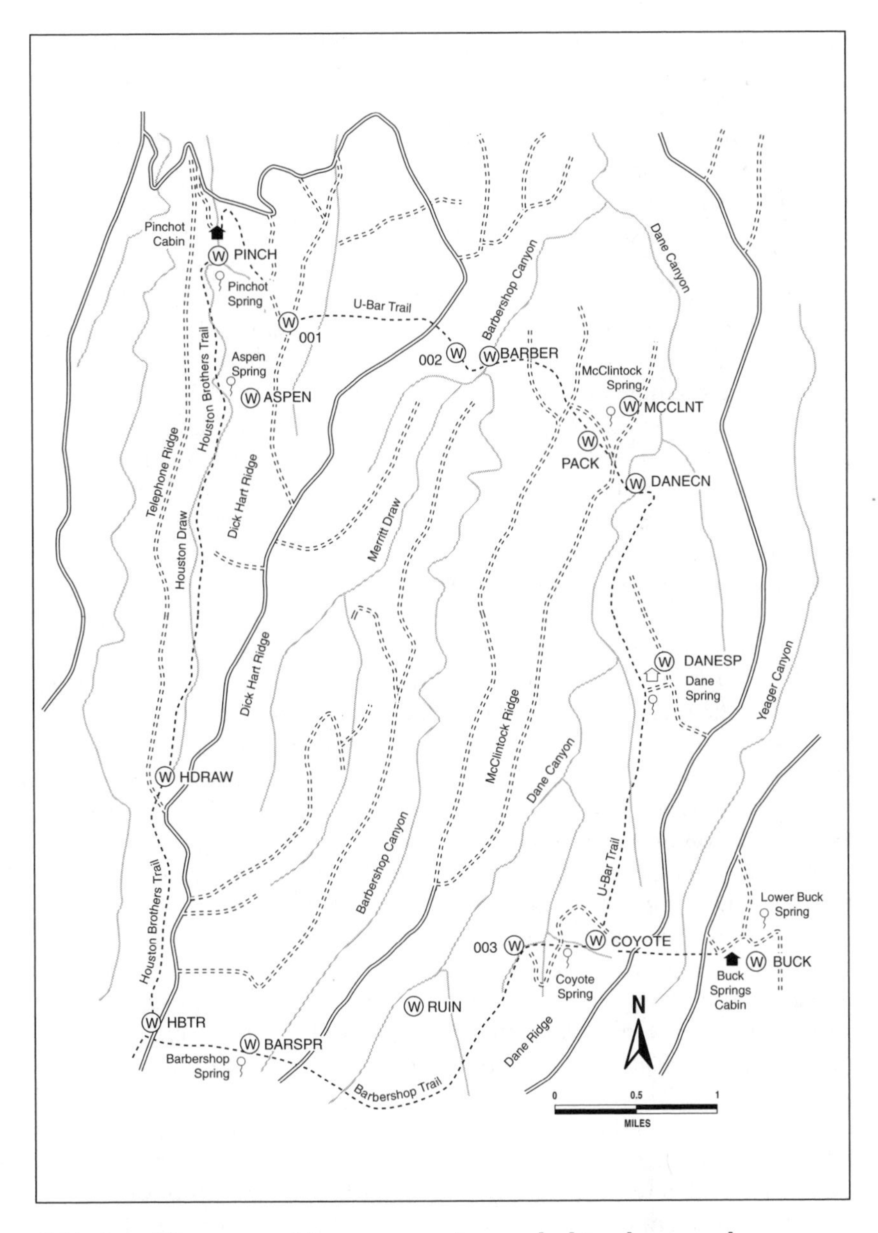

Cabin Loop hike route, with some waypoints marked in advance and others added during hike

the trail entirely. Stopping at the last blazed tree you are able to find, you turn on the receiver and save your position as waypoint 003. After looking at the topographic map, you decide to hike cross-country directly to Barbershop Spring, your planned campsite. The terrain is nearly flat, and you will have only a few shallow canyons to cross. The receiver shows that the BARSPR waypoint is at 243 degrees, 1.9 miles away. You use your compass to check the direction, then set out.

Cross-country travel is easy through the open forest. You have been walking for just over half an hour when, descending into one of the shallow canyons, you spot the ruins of a log cabin alongside the drainage. The old structure is not marked on the topographic map. Checking the area, you cannot find a road or trail leading to the cabin site. You would like to spend some time exploring, but it is late afternoon and time presses, so you save your position on the receiver as a waypoint named RUIN. You also mark the location on your topographic map using the UTM coordinates shown on the display. You plan to return later and use the saved waypoint to find the old cabin.

Resuming your cross-country walk toward Barbershop Spring, you walk for about twenty minutes before checking your progress on the receiver. The spring is now 0.3 mile away, and the map shows that you should be crossing a major dirt road very shortly. You do, but there is still no sign of the trail. On the far side of the road you descend into a shallow canyon; this is probably the head of Barbershop Canyon. The GPS display confirms this hypothesis. As you continue toward the spring, you leave the receiver on. When it shows you already at the spring, you are standing on dry forest floor, but a shallow ravine lies ahead. As you descend into the ravine, you find a faint trail and distinct blazes on the trees leading to the west. You find the spring in the ravine and fill your water bottles. It is a damp, buggy place, and you prefer not to camp near springs anyway, so you hike a few hundred yards west on the trail and find a place to camp out of sight of both the trail and the spring.

The next morning, back on the trail, you check the receiver. The distance and bearing to the junction with the Houston Brothers Trail should be 0.5 mile west, and the receiver confirms that. The trail crosses a road, and you find the junction on the other side. You turn right and hike north. The next waypoint, HDRAW, marks the point where the trail descends into Houston Draw. The trail remains distinct, and you locate the head of the draw without difficulty. Nevertheless, you are glad that you saved the waypoint as a backup.

You know that Pinchot Cabin, the trailhead, is located in Houston Draw, so all you have to do is follow the draw north to reach it. Still, there are few landmarks in the upper part of the draw, so you check your progress on the receiver from time to time. You also want to make sure that you find Aspen Spring. After an hour of steady hiking, you find a spring in an aspen grove. There is no sign, so you use the receiver to confirm that you are really at Aspen Spring. From here it is an easy walk of less than a mile to Pinchot Cabin and the trailhead.

Exploring a Desert Mountain Range

GPS is especially handy when you are hiking or exploring cross-country. In the next example, a cross-country hike in the desert, you want to explore a desert mountain range that looks interesting. According to your topographic map, the nearest access is a dirt road that parallels the range about 10 miles away. The only water source you know of is a natural tank that holds rainwater. Late winter seems to be the ideal time to go. It has been a wet winter, so the tank should be full, and now the weather is dry and cool—perfect for hiking. You plan to take three days on the trip because of the long walk across the desert to reach the foot of the range.

Entering Waypoints in Advance

Because you do not know where you will want to park along the approach road, you cannot place a waypoint in advance. However, you do have a map location for the natural water tank, obtained from a Bureau of Land Management ranger. Finding the water is critical to the success of your trip, so you carefully determine the Universal Transverse Mercator (UTM) coordinates and enter a waypoint called TANK into your GPS receiver. The tank is near the southern end of the section of the range you would like to explore, so you plan to hike to the tank and then explore to the north before returning to your vehicle. Because of the length of the approach drive, you probably will not make it to the tank the first night, so you plan to carry enough water for a dry camp.

Finding Your Starting Point

As you drive along the desert road, you turn on the receiver and set up TANK as a GoTo route. Then you switch to the plot screen and zoom until you can see both your present position and TANK. This allows you to see where you are in relation to the tank. You park your truck where the road makes its closest approach to TANK. Given that your GPS

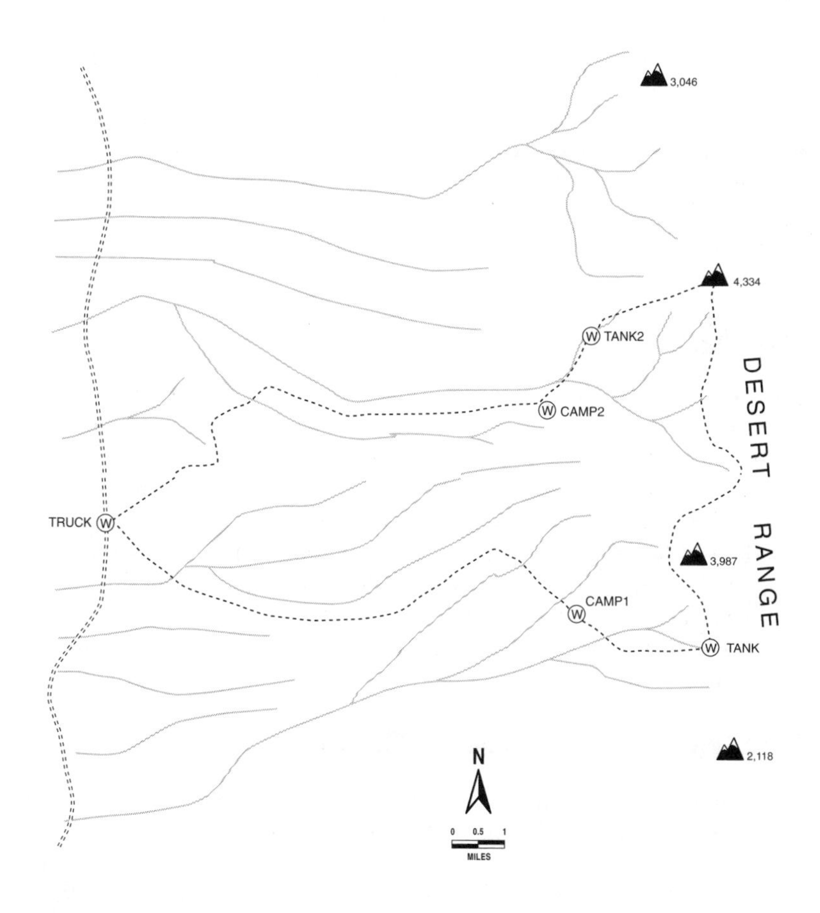

Waypoints for exploring a desert mountain range

receiver has been running continuously on the vehicle's power, you know that it should have a good position fix. After making sure that the receiver is in 3-D navigation mode and that there are no warning messages, you save your position as a waypoint named TRUCK. You also plot your position on your map and write the coordinates on the map margin.

Hiking to Your First Waypoint

Next you check the GPS navigation page, which is still telling you the bearing and distance to the tank. You use your compass to sight along the GPS bearing to the tank, and you note a peak along the crest of the distant range. You will use the peak for general guidance as you cross the desert plain. You stash the GPS receiver and compass in your pack and start hiking. The otherwise flat plain is cut by numerous dry washes, so you constantly make small detours, but focusing on the distant peak keeps you heading in the right direction. As expected, the setting sun forces you to stop and camp just as you reach the foothills. The receiver shows the tank still 2 miles away.

Avoiding Rough Terrain

In the morning you check the GPS bearing to TANK and use your compass to find the direction. The terrain between you and the tank looks rugged, so you skirt it to the south. When you judge that you have gone halfway to the tank, you switch on the receiver, check the bearing and distance, and then hike directly toward the tank. You find it easily, and it is a welcome sight in the otherwise dry canyon. You check that the TANK waypoint is accurately located and then continue north along the range. Since your plan is to hike up to the crest of the range and work your way north to the highest peak, you navigate by the terrain and do not use your receiver.

Marking a New Water Source

After climbing the peak late in the day, you descend the southwest slopes in the general direction of your truck. You have enough water for another dry camp, so you plan to descend to the foothills and look for a campsite. While hiking down a dry wash, you find another natural water tank where the bed drops over a rock ledge. It is smaller than the original tank but worth knowing about, so you turn on your GPS receiver and save your position as a new waypoint, TANK2. You also check your position against nearby landmarks and mark the tank's position on your map. You pick up some extra water and continue another mile or two to camp.

Returning to Your Vehicle

In the morning you use the receiver to determine the direction and distance to your truck. Since there are no landmarks in that direction, you maintain your course using the sun. You are not concerned about maintaining exact direction because you know that the terrain will force you off course anyway. Sure enough, you quickly see that the low ridge you camped on offers the easiest way down. You walk almost directly west and then slightly northwest before the going becomes easier. Taking a break, you again use the receiver to find the direction to your truck. This time you keep the receiver and compass handy as you hike because the desert is nearly flat, and you can see only about half a mile ahead because of the low brush lining the numerous dry washes. You maintain your course with the compass, stopping to check your progress occasionally with the receiver. Soon you spot your truck.

Although this hike certainly could have been done without GPS, satellite navigation made it easier and faster to find the critical water tank. It also freed you to explore at will along the range, knowing that you could descend out of the mountains and hike directly to your vehicle at any time. Without GPS you would have had to keep track of your position carefully and deliberately hike toward a point well to one side of your truck so that you would know which way to turn when you hit the road. Finally, with GPS, you were able to mark the exact location of the second water tank; having this information will make it easier to explore the northern section of the range on a later trip.

Mapping a Mountain Bike Trail

In this example you will use a GPS receiver with a data cable and a personal computer with National Geographic's Topo! software and maps. The object is to help your local mountain bike club plan and map a new bike trail in cooperation with the state park service. The proposed trail wanders through dense forest with few landmarks. The park service wants a map of the proposed route before it is constructed and a final, detailed map of the trail after it is constructed. The club also wants a good map of the trail for its members and other riders.

Planning the Trail

Your plan is to start the trail from a gravel road and run it through the forest to a viewpoint. On your personal computer, you use Topo! to display a map of the proposed route. Then, using the "Handheld | New GPS Route" menu selection, you create a new GPS route. You name it VIEWTRAIL in the route editor that pops up. The route is automatically activated—any new waypoints that you create will be entered into it. You select "Tool | Waypoint" from the menu and left-click the mouse on the proposed start of the trail segment. A waypoint properties sheet pops up; you name the first waypoint START.

You want to run the trail across a series of drainages to create a "roller coaster" section that is fun but not too technical. After studying the map, you mark a couple of appropriate waypoints. You let Topo! automatically name them 001 and 002. You want the last segment of the trail to run along a flat ridge out to the viewpoint, so you create another waypoint called 003. A final waypoint, VPOINT, marks your destination—the viewpoint. You save the waypoints and route on your computer as ViewPointTrail.TPO.

Downloading Data

You connect the GPS receiver to your computer. After setting Topo! to use your specific receiver, you download the route and waypoints using the "Handheld | Export" menu selection. This takes just a couple of seconds. You also print the map.

In the Field

You use the GoTo function on your receiver to navigate directly to START. That way, as you drive the approach road through the dense forest, you will know when you have reached the proposed start of the trail. When you arrive at START, you see right away that it is not a good trailhead because there is no place to park. You passed a section of road with a wide shoulder about half a mile back, so you turn around. As you expected, there is room for several cars to park, so you stop the car, grab your pack, turn on your GPS receiver, and save your location as a waypoint named PARK.

Mapping the Proposed Trail

You need a section of trail to connect PARK to the rest of the planned trail, so after looking at the map you decide to check out the area to the right of the road. A few hundred yards of thrashing your way through deadfall and brush convinces you that the bike club will kill you if you route the trail there. You check out the left side of the road. It is much better—the forest is fairly open, and the terrain is just right for an easy roller-coaster trail. You save a waypoint, letting the receiver name it 004.

Now you need to connect waypoint 004 to the rest of the planned trail. You use the GoTo function to navigate directly to 001, the first waypoint on the original planned trail. As you work your way through the forest, you mark key points with several more waypoints—005 through 009—including the place where you cross the road beyond START. When you reach 001, you activate the VIEWTRAIL route. This starts navigation to 002. As you go, you mark more key points where you want the trail to run. You use your receiver's position-averaging feature to make the waypoints as accurate as possible, and then you enter them into the existing route. By the time you reach VPOINT, you have created waypoints 010 through 014 to mark the rest of the proposed trail.

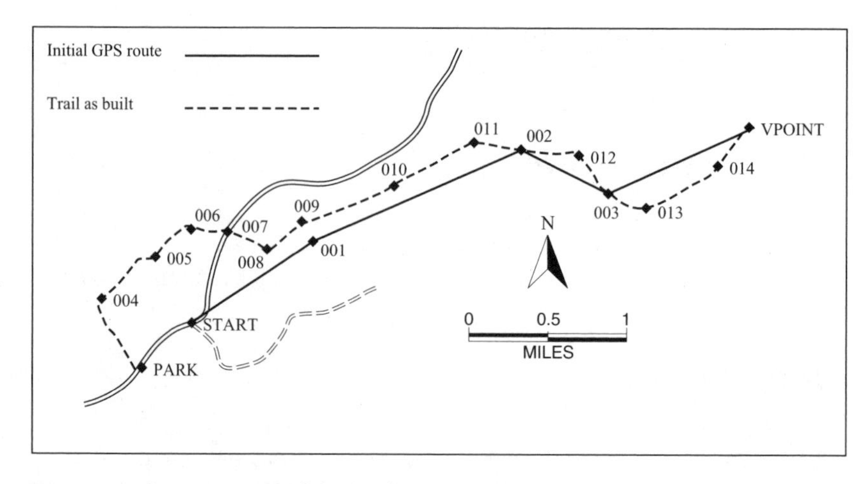

Waypoints for a mountain bike trail

Uploading the Field Waypoints

Back at home, you upload all of the waypoints from the GPS receiver to your computer, then use the Topo! freehand route tool to draw in the trail along the waypoints. This gives you a provisional map to print for the park rangers. Before printing it, you delete the START waypoint to avoid confusion about the trailhead and save the file.

Creating the Final Route

After the state park service approves the route, you use the Topo! GPS route tool to create a new route on your computer with all of your field waypoints; you call this route APPROVEDTRAIL to distinguish it from your original planned trail. Then you copy and paste all of the waypoints into the route to create the final map for trail construction. After deleting the old VIEWTRAIL route, you activate the APPROVEDTRAIL route, save the file, download the route and waypoints to your GPS receiver, and print the map.

In the field it is easy to navigate along the APPROVEDTRAIL route. You mark the trail with flags for the club members to follow while the trail is under construction.

Mapping the Constructed Trail

After the trail is complete, you ride it with your GPS receiver and save as many waypoints as you need to map each twist and turn. You also use a cyclometer to measure distances between key points on the trail. After uploading the waypoints to your computer, you create a final map for both club riders and the park service. Of course, the park service is so impressed with your trail-planning ability that it immediately asks for your assistance with another trail project.

Relocating Your Favorite Fishing Spot

Before doing any water travel with GPS, learn how to use your receiver's man overboard (MOB) function, if it has one. When activated, this feature instantly saves a waypoint and then starts navigation to that waypoint. Although it is intended for larger boats that take some time and distance to maneuver back to the marked point, the MOB function can be useful for lake paddlers and anglers, too. To be useful, MOB should be activated with a button on the receiver, not be buried deep in a menu system.

For flatwater navigation, it helps to mount your receiver so that you can check it easily. You do not need to leave it on all the time; you can just turn it on for position and course checks. You will want to have a fully waterproof receiver, but if you do not, buy a special waterproof bag (made specifically for handheld receivers) with a transparent cover. It is harder to operate the receiver through the bag, but you can secure the bag to the boat or your gear. If the receiver does fall in the water, the bag will keep it dry and afloat.

Planning the Route

Let's say that you want to paddle your canoe across a large lake to reach a favorite fishing spot and campsite on the far side. The distance is about 5 miles, and there are no landmarks on the far shore to steer by. Last time you were there, you saved a waypoint called FISH at the spot. Before setting out, save your launching point as a waypoint called LAUNCH; then create and activate a route from LAUNCH to FISH. As you paddle, the navigation page shows the bearing and distance to your goal. You can use the track information to stay on course, turning until your track and the bearing agree, but an easier method is to use the course deviation indicator (CDI), located on one of your navigation pages. This CDI is usually a horizontal row of dots with a vertical bar or arrow. (Some receivers use a graphic of a road with a symbol representing your position.) The bar moves left or right to show how far off course you are. You can change the scale of the CDI in the setup page. The CDI is not used much for land travel but can be very helpful for direct travel by water or air.

Using the Course Deviation Indicator

Set the CDI to its most sensitive scale. When you are on course, the course marker stays centered. If you get off course, the marker moves to the side. To correct any deviation, make a small change in your heading and see if the CDI starts to center. If not, make another small heading change. When the CDI starts to move toward center, hold that heading until it has centered. If you make large changes, you probably will find yourself zigzagging through your course.

Cross Track Error

The cross track error (XTK) display shows distance off course. You can use XTK to help you decide how far to turn to get back on course. For example, if your destination is 5 miles away and your XTK is 0.1 mile, make a 10-degree turn to get back on course. If your XTK is 1 mile and you have 5 miles to go, turn 30 degrees to get back on course. The idea is to get back on course without going too far out of your way.

Effects of Wind and Current

If you have wind or current from one side, you will be carried off course even though your heading is the same as the bearing to the waypoint. In this case, steer a few degrees into the wind or current to compensate. Check the CDI occasionally; if you are off course, adjust your heading toward your desired course. If the wind or current is steady, you will be able to find a heading that will keep you exactly on course, so that you paddle the shortest distance to your destination.

Estimated Time of Arrival

It can be difficult to judge distance on water, but the estimated time of arrival (ETA) display can help measure your progress. Remember that ETA is based on your speed made good and the distance remaining to your waypoint. If you frequently wander off course or slow down, your ETA will change.

Keep in mind that the heading and ETA displays may be inaccurate at low speeds on some receivers; do not make constant course changes in response to small changes in the display. If a distant landmark is available, steer by it to stay on course; otherwise, use a compass.

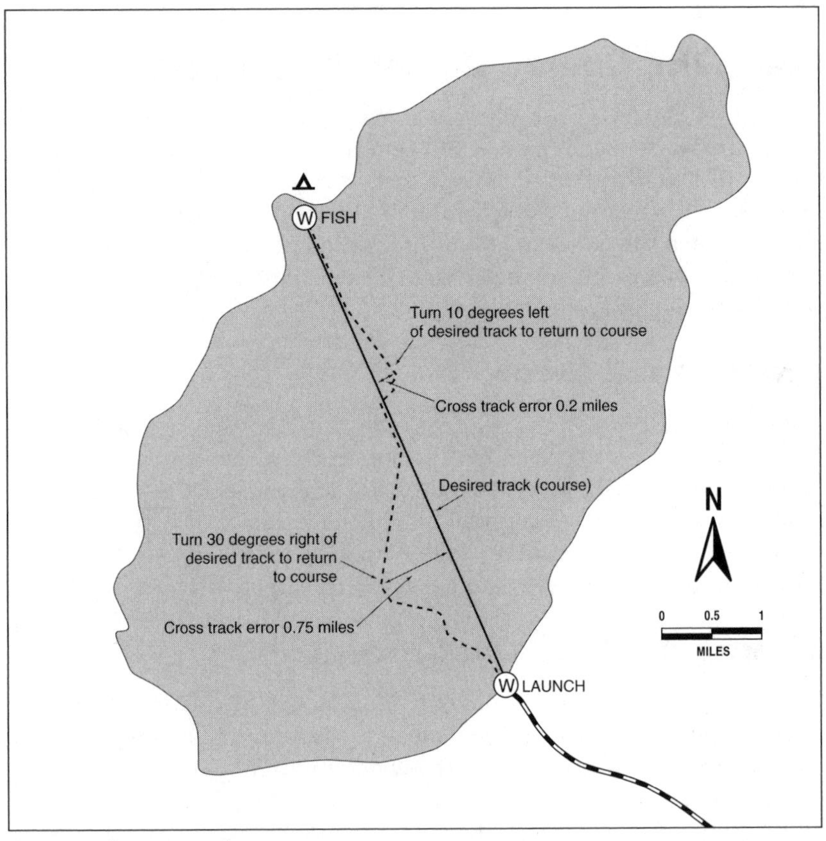

Cross track error on the water

Advanced GPS

GPS offers additional features that are likely to be of interest to backcountry users: the Automatic Position Reporting System (APRS), Differential GPS (DGPS), and the Wide Area Augmentation System (WAAS). In addition, the U.S. military is testing battlefield spoofing and jamming systems designed to disrupt an enemy's ability to use GPS. Other applications for GPS, such as surveying and land management, are beyond the scope of this book. Refer to the appendix for books on these subjects.

The Automatic Position Reporting System

APRS is an amateur radio system that uses digital radio to track objects. APRS stations can be fixed, mobile, or portable, so the system can track all types of vehicles and even people. Since the system uses radio communications, it can transmit general messages as well as specialized information. The Internet also can be used to link APRS stations, so an amateur radio license is not required for those who use the system. An APRS station uses a computer to display a map with the positions of all other APRS stations. Weather data and message traffic also can be displayed.

Amateur radio operators are using APRS to provide communications and position tracking in disaster situations and for public service events such as races and parades. The Civil Air Patrol uses APRS to help it search for overdue aircraft. For more information, visit www.aprs.net.

Differential GPS

Each GPS satellite transmits three primary navigation signals: the coarse/acquisition code (C/A), the precise code (P), and the navigation signal. Your receiver uses this information to compute its position. Errors creep into the calculated position because of small errors in the satellite positions, variations in radio wave propagation through the atmosphere, and other factors. DGPS overcomes most of these inaccuracies by using a GPS receiver and a DGPS beacon transmitter placed on a known, surveyed point. The transmitter continuously computes the difference between its known position and its GPS position, and it transmits the correction. Field GPS receivers equipped with a DGPS receiver pick up this signal and correct their location accordingly. The accuracy is 16 feet or better.

DGPS is more complex and costly than the basic system because a DGPS beacon receiver must be attached to the normal GPS receiver. The system works only within range of a DGPS beacon transmitter.

DGPS is routinely used in surveying and will become increasingly important in navigation. The U.S. Coast Guard maintains a network of DGPS stations to improve the accuracy of marine navigation near the coast. The U.S. Forest Service, the U.S. Bureau of Land Management, other federal agencies, and private citizens use DGPS locally to improve the accuracy of their survey and mapping operations.

The Wide Area Augmentation System

The Federal Aviation Administration (FAA) built WAAS, a differential GPS system, to improve the accuracy of GPS for aircraft between destinations. The FAA uses a similar system, the Local Area Augmentation System (LAAS), for precision instrument approaches—to help aircraft find a runway in bad weather, for example. Tests have demonstrated an LAAS accuracy of better than 1 inch. Another function of both WAAS and LAAS is to warn flight crews of degraded accuracy or GPS failure. Such warnings are critical when GPS is used to guide a fast-moving aircraft to within a few feet of a runway.

WAAS consists of a series of geostationary satellites located over the equator and ground reference stations that cover North America. The system transmits on current GPS frequencies, so it is available to anyone with a receiver capable of using WAAS information. Such receivers have an accuracy of 3 to 5 meters (10 to 16 feet) horizontally and 3 to 7 meters (10 to 23 feet) vertically. Although backcountry users do not really need this degree of accuracy, many handheld receivers are now WAAS-enabled. Because of their position over the equator, WAAS satellites appear low in the southern sky for many North American users. Generally, you must be airborne or on open water, where there is a low horizon, to receive the correction signals. Look at your receiver's satellite status page to determine whether it is accessing WAAS information.

New Military Applications

The military has been testing a battlefield spoofing and jamming system that would deny an enemy the benefits of GPS. Spoofing a GPS receiver fools it into giving false positions, while jamming prevents it from displaying any position at all.

The Future of GPS

GPS grew out of the military's need for an accurate, twenty-four-hour, global, all-weather navigation system that could provide rapidly updated positions for ships, aircraft, tanks, troops, and weapons. When planning for the system started in 1973, there were several major goals. The system had to be resistant to jamming, and it had to be encrypted (i.e., the radio signals had to be encoded) so that unauthorized persons could not interfere with it. The system also needed to be passive so that users would not have to reveal their positions by transmitting. In addition, the U.S. Congress wanted the Department of Defense to consolidate all of the existing military navigation systems into one. Civilian uses were not part of the original design, but many of the design features that make the system so useful to the military also make it attractive to civilians. The passive design means that GPS receivers are relatively simple devices, and their cost has dropped rapidly as electronic and computer technology improves.

The first GPS satellite, NAVSTAR 1, was launched in 1978; its ten sisters followed over the next few years. These early satellites were prototypes, designed to test and refine the system. Though their design life was four-and-a-half years, some lasted more than twice that long. The next generation of GPS satellites was launched in 1989. These satellites are hardened against attack by antisatellite weapons and are designed to last seven-and-a-half years. A third generation of GPS satellites have more accurate atomic clocks and use intersatellite communications to reduce dependency on updates from ground stations.

In the future, GPS technology will become commonplace. Some people are concerned that GPS and other technologies, such as cell and satellite telephones, degrade or even destroy the wilderness experience. It is not a new argument. The same concern arose when the lightweight, high-tech aluminum pack frame was invented, and ham radio has generated similar complaints. I am a lifetime amateur radio operator, and I have carried a small ham radio receiver in my pack for many years. Some of my hiking companions have objected to the intrusion of two-way radio communications into our trips. The answer, as always, is to use technology appropriately during your backcountry trip. When I hike with non-ham companions, I leave the radio out of sight in my pack, for use only in an emergency. Likewise, you can keep a GPS receiver in reserve in case your party becomes disoriented—much the way some people always carry a compass but rarely use it in open country.

Be careful not to become dependent on gadgets to get you out of trouble in wild country. In some areas—Utah's canyon country, for example, where the terrain is cut by thousands of canyons—GPS and compass navigation are utterly useless. Although a GPS receiver will tell you the direction and distance to your destination in a straight line, to get there you may have to hike many more miles and work closely with the terrain and a map to avoid canyons and other obstacles. Lastly, remember that electronic devices fail. Plan to rely on your own survival knowledge in the backcountry and use your high-tech equipment only as a backup.

Appendix: Resources

GPS Companies

Adventure GPS Products
1629 Fourth Avenue Southeast
Decatur, AL 35601
(888) 477-4386, (256) 351-2151
www.gps4fun.com; info@gps4fun.com (e-mail)

GPS City
6 Sunset Way, Suite 108
Henderson, NV 89014
(866) GPS-CITY, (702) 990-5600
www.gpscity.com; sales@gpscity.com (e-mail)

GPS Store
P.O. Box 7659
Shallotte, NC 28470
(888) 477-2611, (910) 575-9544
www.thegpsstore.com; info@thegpsstore.com (e-mail)

Map World
3191 Sports Arena Boulevard, Suite F
San Diego, CA 92110
(619) 291-3830
www.mapworld.com; maps@mapworld.com (e-mail)

Navtech Seminars and GPS Supply
6121 Lincolnia Road, Suite 400
Alexandria, VA 22312-2707
(800) 628-0885, (703) 256-8900
www.navtechgps.com; gpsteach@navtechgps.com (e-mail)

GPS Manufacturers

Eagle Electronics
P.O. Box 669
Catoosa, OK 74015-0669
(800) 324-1354, (918) 437-6881
www.eaglegps.com

Garmin International, Inc.
1200 East 151st Street
Olathe, KS 66062
(913) 397-8200
www.garmin.com

Lowrance Electronics
12000 East Skelly Drive
Tulsa, OK 74128
(800) 324-1356
www.lowrance.com

Magellan Systems Inc.
960 Overland Court
San Dimas, CA 91773
(909) 394-5000
www.magellangps.com

Raytheon Marine
22 Cotton Road, Unit D
Nashua, NH 03063
(800) 539-5539, (603) 881-5200
www.raymarine.com

Si-Tex Marine Electronics, Inc.
11001 Roosevelt Boulevard, Suite 800
St. Petersburg, FL 33716
(727) 576-5734
www.si-tex.com

Trimble Navigation Limited
1440 Lakefront Circle, Suite 110
The Woodlands, TX 77380-3607
(800) 865-4849, (281) 363-4700
www.trimble.com; sales_info@trimble.com (e-mail)

Compass Companies

Brunton Co.
620 East Monroe Avenue
Riverton, WY 82501
(800) 443-4871, (307) 856-6559
www.brunton.com; info@brunton.com (e-mail)

Silva USA
(800) 572-8822
www.silvacompass.com; camping@johnsonoutdoors.com (e-mail)

Suunto USA Inc.
2151 Las Palmas Drive
Carlsbad, CA 92009
(800) 543-9124, (760) 931-6788
www.suuntousa.com; info@suuntousa.com (e-mail)

Map and Map Software Companies

National Geographic Maps (Topo! Maps)
(800) 962-1643
http://maps.nationalgeographic.com/topo

Northport Systems Inc. (Fugawi map software)
95 St. Clair Avenue West, Suite 1406
Toronto, Ontario M4V 1N6, Canada
(416) 920-9300
www.fugawi.com; sales@fugawi.com (e-mail)

DeLorme (Street Atlas USA, Topo USA)
2 DeLorme Drive, P.O. Box 298
Yarmouth, ME 04096
(800) 561-5105
www.delorme.com; info@delorme.com (e-mail)

U.S. Geological Survey, Information Services
Box 25286
Denver, CO 80225
(800) HELP-MAP
http://mapping.usgs.gov

UnderTow Software, Inc.
26011 West Lauren Drive
Channahon, IL 60410
(800) 257-9244, (815) 521-9950
www.undertowsoftware.com

GPS Books

Ferguson, Michael. *GPS Land Navigation.* Boise: Glassford Publishing, 1997.
A detailed explanation of GPS, maps, and coordinate systems.

Greenhood, David. *Mapping.* Chicago: University of Chicago Press, 1973.
Very readable coverage of coordinate systems, map projections, and map making.

Hofmann-Wellenhof, B., Herbert Lichtenegger, and James Collins. *Global Positioning System: Theory and Practice.* New York: Springer-Verlag, 2001.
A comprehensive and technical look at GPS.

Kals, William S. *Land Navigation Handbook: The Sierra Club Guide to Map and Compass.* San Francisco: Sierra Club Books, 1983.
Probably the best coverage of classic backcountry navigation using a map, compass, and altimeter.

Kjellström, Björn. *Be Expert with Map and Compass.* New York: John Wiley & Sons, 1994.
A classic work on orienteering, a competitive sport in which people use a map and compass to find preset marks on an orienteering course. Much of the information applies to backcountry navigation as well.

Larijani, L. Casey. *GPS for Everyone.* Chicago: Independent Publishers Group, 1998.
A general survey of GPS and its uses.

Logston, Tom. *The Navstar Global Positioning System.* New York: Van Nostrand Reinhold, 1992.
A good overview of GPS.

Sickle, Jan Van. *GPS for Land Surveyors.* 2nd ed. Boca Raton, FL: CRC Press, 2001.
A moderately technical explanation of GPS and precision land survey.

GPS Magazine

GPS World
P.O. Box 10488
Eugene, OR 97440
www.gpsworld.com/gpsworld; info@gpsworld.com (e-mail)

Index

About the Author

Bruce Grubbs is an avid hiker, mountain biker, paddler, and cross-country skier who has been exploring the American West for more than 30 years. He has used high-technology gear in the backcountry in his work as a professional pilot, an amateur radio operator, and a mountain rescue team member. Bruce holds Airline Transport Pilot and Instrument Flight Instructor certificates. He lives in Flagstaff, Arizona, and is the author of more than fifteen FalconGuides.